# NEW MERMAIDS

General editors:
William C. Carroll, Boston University
Brian Gibbons, University of Münster
Tiffany Stern, University of Oxford

- villian as protagonist
- he's an underdog
  because he's a jew
  ↓
  not his
  choice

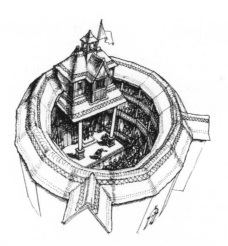

Reconstruction of an Elizabethan Theatre
by C. Walter Hodges

# NEW MERMAIDS

NEW MERMAIDS

CHRISTOPHER MARLOWE

# THE JEW OF MALTA

Edited by James R. Siemon
Boston University

Bloomsbury Methuen Drama
An imprint of Bloomsbury Publishing Plc

B L O O M S B U R Y
LONDON · OXFORD · NEW YORK · NEW DELHI · SYDNEY

**Bloomsbury Methuen Drama**

An imprint of Bloomsbury Publishing Plc

Imprint previously known as Methuen Drama

| 50 Bedford Square | 1385 Broadway |
|---|---|
| London | New York |
| WC1B 3DP | NY 10018 |
| UK | USA |

**www.bloomsbury.com**

**BLOOMSBURY, METHUEN DRAMA and the Diana logo are
trademarks of Bloomsbury Publishing Plc**

First New Mermaid edition published 1966
© Ernest Benn Limited 1966

Second edition published 1994
© A & C Black Publishers Limited 1994

This third edition with a new introduction published 2009
Reprinted by Bloomsbury Methuen Drama 2011, 2013 (twice), 2014, 2015 (twice)

© A & C Black Publishers Limited 2009

**British Library Cataloguing-in-Publication Data**
A catalogue record for this book is available from the British Library.

ISBN: PB: 978-0-7136-7766-9
ePDF: 978-1-4081-4489-3
ePUB: 978-1-4081-4490-9

**Library of Congress Cataloging-in-Publication Data**
A catalog record for this book is available from the Library of Congress.

Series: New Mermaids

Printed and bound in India

# CONTENTS

# ACKNOWLEDGEMENTS

It is a pleasure to acknowledge the help and encouragement of colleagues, friends and students. From early to late, Professor Brian Gibbons offered suggestions and enthusiastic support. Professor David Bevington shared his knowledge and insight at a particularly important time in the evolution of the project. Professor Emily Bartels read over the introduction and generously allowed me to read her work in progress. And, with characteristic generosity, Professor William Carroll provided help and prevented more than a few errors. Students in my classes in Renaissance drama at Boston University provided a never-failing stimulus to further thinking about *The Jew of Malta* and, particularly, to consideration of the issues it raises for our own day.

JAMES R. SIEMON

FOR
RUTH A. SIEMON
AND
RALPH M. SIEMON

# INTRODUCTION

## The Author

In 1564 Christopher Marlowe was born to the Canterbury family of John Marlowe, a shoe-maker who would hold positions of professional and civic authority, but who was sued for nonpayment of debts and rent.[1] Marlowe entered King's School in 1578, and won a scholarship. In 1580 he enrolled at Corpus Christi College, Cambridge, with an Archbishop Parker scholarship. He received the B.A. in 1584; thereafter, his absences occasioned rumours that he had fled to the Catholic seminary in Rheims. The Privy Council defended him, ordering the granting of his M.A. in 1587, insisting that he had done 'good service . . . touching the benefit of his country'. He was evidently involved in international intrigue at the very highest official level, but he was also writing poetry and drama. Marlowe's translations of Ovid's *Amores* and Lucan's *Civil Wars* and *Dido Queen of Carthage* (based on Virgil's *Aeneid*) were probably written before his move to London and the enormous success of *Tamburlaine I* and *II* in 1587–8.

Between 1587 and his murder on 30 May 1593, Marlowe wrote four more plays and the epyllion *Hero and Leander*, saw *Tamburlaine* printed (1590) and got arrested five times. He shared a room with the playwright Thomas Kyd in 1591, and by February 1592 *The Jew of Malta*, which frequently echoes Kyd's *The Spanish Tragedy*, was being performed. No record authenticates performance of *Edward II* before the end of 1592 or of *Doctor Faustus* before Marlowe's death. *The Jew of Malta* (1591?) probably follows *Tamburlaine* in composition and precedes the other two plays. In January 1593 Philip Henslowe, financier of the Rose theatre, records *The Massacre at Paris* as 'ne', i.e., new to performance or newly revised.

Marlowe was arrested in 1589 for involvement in the quarrel that led to the killing of William Bradley by the poet Thomas Watson. During his brief imprisonment, he became acquainted with the gentleman counterfeiter and Catholic activist, John Poole. Marlowe was arrested three times in 1592: in January at the report of co-conspirator Richard Baines, for counterfeiting in the Dutch town of Flushing, a centre of espionage; in May for threatening a constable and beadle in London; and in September for assault in Canterbury. No substantial penalty resulted. Lord Treasurer

---

1 What follows is based on David Riggs, *The World of Christopher Marlowe*, 2004; David Riggs, 'The Poet in the Play: Life and Art in *Tamburlaine* and *The Jew of Malta*' in *Shakespeare, Marlowe, Jonson: New Directions in Biography*, ed. Takashi Kozuka and J.R. Mulryne, 2006, 205–24; William Urry, *Christopher Marlowe and Canterbury*, 1988. See also Constance Brown Kuriyama, *Christopher Marlowe: A Renaissance Life*, 2002.

Burghley released him from the capital counterfeiting charge. However, amid concerns about religious division, the Privy Council ordered Marlowe's arrest in 1593. Having been charged with blasphemy and atheism by Thomas Kyd (himself undergoing investigation and torture) and the informer Richard Baines, Marlowe appeared on 20 May before the Council and was ordered to report daily.[2] On 30 May he was invited to a Deptford tavern by three men, two of whom had participated in clandestine activities. He was stabbed through the eye socket, dying instantly. The coroner's jury ruled his killer, Ingram Frizer, acted in self-defence. Marlowe was buried 1 June 1593, at the Church of St Nicholas, Deptford. Frizer received a royal pardon two weeks later.

By the time of his death, Marlowe had acquired a wide, but dichotomous, reputation. Despite successful plays and acclaim from George Peele (who called him the 'Muses darling'), appreciation for him, like that exhibited in *The Second Part of the Return from Parnassus*, is mixed with strong moral disapproval:

> *Marlowe* was happy in his buskined muse,
> Alas unhappy in his life and end.
> Pitty it is that wit so ill should dwell,
> Wit lent from heaven, but vices sent from hell.[3]

Contemporaries invoked atheism, disrespect for authority, cruelty, violence and Machiavellian policy in characterizing the man. These terms suggest aspects of Marlowe's works – cosmic irony, sardonic humour, intellectual aspiration, spectacular violence, impassioned verse and detached analysis – which have won four hundred years of increasingly positive response.[4]

2  See Paul H. Kocher *Christopher Marlowe: A Study of His Thought, Learning, and Character*, 1946, pp. 33–68; and R.B. Wernham, 'Christopher Marlowe at Flushing in 1592', *English Historical Review* 91 (1976), 344–5.

3  Cited from Millar Maclure, ed., *Marlowe: The Critical Heritage 1588–1896*, 1979, p. 46.

4  Annotated bibliographies of Marlowe criticism include: Jonathan F.S. Post, 'Recent Studies in Marlowe (1968–1976)', *ELR* 7 (1977), 382–99; Kenneth Friedenreich, *Christopher Marlowe: An Annotated Bibliography since 1950* (1979); Ronald Levao, 'Recent Studies in Marlowe (1977–1986)', *ELR* 18 (1988), 329–42; Bruce E. Brandt, *Christopher Marlowe in the Eighties: An Annotated Bibliography*, 1992; Patrick Cheney, 'Recent Studies in Marlowe (1987–1998)', *ELR* 31 (2001), 288–328.

# Date and Sources

The Prologue mentions the Duke of Guise (assassinated December 1588) as 'now' dead; Philip Henslowe's account of daily productions at the Rose playhouse, his 'diary', records performances beginning 26 February 1592. Composition is thought to have taken place between 1589 and 1591. Henslowe records some thirty-six performances between 26 February 1592 and 21 June 1596, allowing for an interim from July 1592 to December 1593 during which the London theatres were closed. This indicates that the play was initially popular: ten profitable performances between February and June 1592, revival in the month of playing allowed during the closing, and performances in 1594, 1596 and in 1601, when Henslowe records purchasing 'divers thinge[s] for the Jewe of malta'.[5]

Unlike Marlowe's other plays, this has no single source.[6] However, *The Jew of Malta* is filled with allusions and engages in dialogues with contemporary issues and discourses. History contributed the famous 1565 Turkish siege of Christian Malta that loosely provides the setting along with potentially interesting ambiguities. The failed siege of Malta was understood as a victory of Christianity over Islam, but it also occasioned rumours of financial complicity between Jews and Turks, responding to aggressive raiding by Malta's Knights that had made Malta an infamous market for enslaved captives.[7] Some have asserted relationships between Barabas and a historical Jew, either Joseph Nasi, a Jewish financier, appointed Duke of the Island of Naxos by Selim, son of Sultan Suleiman II, and an agent of the Ottoman empire; or David Passi, a self-serving double-agent of Constantinople, whose greed, betrayal and sudden downfall were the stuff of 1591 reports from Venice.[8]

Jews who practiced their faith had been banished from England since the thirteenth century and would not be readmitted, except as converts, until 1656, but *The Jew of Malta* draws upon widely-shared discourses of European anti-semitism. Although there is some evidence of covert worship among London's Jewish population, the inherited English prejudice, unlike its Continental varieties, lacked a genuine local object upon which to vent itself.[9] Nevertheless, the English stage frequently referred to Jews

---

5 See *Henslowe's Diary*, ed. RA. Foakes, 2nd edition 2002, p. 170.
6 For sources and analogues, see *Christopher Marlowe: The Plays and their Sources*, ed. Vivien Thomas and William Tydeman, 1994; rpt. 1999, 295–337.
7 On the siege, see Brian Blouet, *The Story of Malta*, 1967; for rumours that Suleiman financed the siege with loans from Jewish bankers, see p. 53; compare Cecil Roth, 'The Jews of Malta', *TJHSE* 12 (1928–31), 187–251, p. 216.
8 For references to Nasi, alias Joao or Juan Miguez, see Cecil Roth, *The House of Nasi: The Duke of Naxos*, 1948.
9 The category of 'Jew' in sixteenth-century England is a complex construct, with political,

and Judaism, and, in fact, the prosecution of Queen Elizabeth's Jewish physician, Dr Roderigo Lopez, in 1594, may have contributed to the popularity of *The Jew of Malta* and of Shakespeare's *The Merchant of Venice* (1598?).[10] No surviving Elizabethan dramas treat Jewish protagonists as extensively. Robert Wilson's morality play, *The Three Ladies of London* (1584?), provides an exceptionally 'positive' portrayal which is perhaps relevant because its Turkish Jew exposes money-grubbing Christian hypocrisy. The language of the stage – like that of Elizabethan culture generally – routinely associated Jews with diabolical opposition to Christianity, cruelty (even ritual cannibalism and mass poisoning), treachery, usury, avarice, legalism, sharp practice, tribalism and physical repulsiveness.[11] There is also a larger European context derived from contacts with Jews who traded, gathered intelligence and were sometimes associated with Ottoman interests in the Mediterranean region.[12] Marlowe's play draws on the anti-Semitic inheritance as well as contemporary suspicions in constructing Barabas, but the ends to which this material is put will require further discussion.

The play's other sorts of allusions have varied sources. Its many proverbs, like its classical allusions, are always loaded with implication; for

theological, economic and moral dimensions. Professing Jews were banished from England from 1290 to 1656, but so-called 'new Christians' or Marranos – outward converts, usually of Portuguese origin – inhabited England throughout the intervening period. On Jewish communities, some apparently practicing their religion secretly, see Lucien Wolf, 'Jews in Elizabethan England', *TJHSE* 11 (1924–7), 1–91; Cecil Roth, 'The Middle Period of Anglo-Jewish History (1290–1655) Reconsidered', *TJHSE* 19 (1955–9), 1–12, and his *History of the Jews in England*, 1964; Harold Pollins, *Economic History of the Jews in England*, 1982; David S. Katz, *The Jews in the History of England, 1485–1850*, 1994; compare the case described by Alan Stewart in 'Mediterranean Trade' (*Remapping the Mediterranean World*, ed. Goram V. Stanivukovic, 2007, pp. 171–3). For positive Elizabethan attitudes towards Judaism, see Theodore K. Rabb, 'The Stirrings of the 1590s and the Return of the Jews to England', *TJHSE* 26 (1974–8), 26–33; also David S. Katz, *Philo-Semitism and the Readmission of the Jews to England 1603–1655*, 1982.

10  See John Gwyer, 'The Case of Dr Lopez', *TJHSE* 16 (1945–51), 163–84. For staging of the plays during the Lopez period, see Roslyn Knutson, 'Influence of the Repertory System on the Revival and Revision of *The Spanish Tragedy* and *Dr Faustus*', *ELR* 18 (1988), 257–74. For Shakespeare's and Marlowe's plays in relation to one another, see Thomas Cartelli, 'Shakespeare's *Merchant*, Marlowe's *Jew*: The Problem of Cultural Difference', *ShakS* 20 (1988), 255-60; James Shapiro, 'Which is *The Merchant* Here, and Which *The Jew*?', *ShakS* 20 (1988), 269–82.

11  In 1579 Stephen Gosson mentions a lost play, *The Jew*, as illustrating 'the greediness of worldly chusers and bloody minds of usurers' (Chambers, *Elizabethan Stage*, 4 vols., 1923, IV, p. 204). For such charges, see James Shapiro, *Shakespeare and the Jews*, 1996, esp. pp. 92–130.

12  See Daniel Vitkus, *Turning Turk: English Theatre and the Multicultural Mediterranean*, 2003, esp. pp. 163–98.

example, see the end of the first scene with its proverbial wisdom about violence (I.i.131; see Tilley, N 321) and self-interest (I.i.185; see Tilley, N 57); its classical references to Iphigenia (I.i.137) and quotations from Ovid (I.i.106–10) and, in Latin, from Terence (I.i.188). Biblical allusions are everywhere, and also powerfully ironic, as, for example, when Barabas dismisses Job's trials as lesser than his own (I.ii.182–99) or when his confrontation with official Malta echoes Christ's passion (I.ii.97–125). [13] The play also employs elements from older drama, like the Croxton Play of the Sacrament, or from contemporary drama, like Thomas Kyd's *Spanish Tragedy*, or from Marlowe's own works (see Ithamore's parodic verses).[14] The most obvious allusion is the invocation of Niccolò Machiavelli.

It is difficult to reconcile Marlowe's 'Machevill', who opens the play, or the action which follows with the actual writings of Machiavelli. There are two difficulties: Machiavelli treats religion as vital to statecraft, while Machevill dismisses it as a 'childish toy'; Machiavelli says nothing about economics, while Machevill claims Barabas has amassed a fortune by Machevill's 'means'.[15] Marlowe's distortion of Machiavelli derives from popular anti-Machiavellian polemic exemplified by Innocent Gentillet's *Anti-Machiavel* (1576); how Marlowe treats that polemical bogeyman will require attention.[16]

13 For Marlowe's strategic allusions, see Judith Weil, *Christopher Marlowe: Merlin's Prophet*, 1977.
14 On Marlowe's indebtedness to morality play structure, see David Bevington, *From Mankind to Marlowe*, 1962, pp. 218–33; for the play's innovations, see Ruth Lunney, *Marlowe and the Popular Tradition*, 2002, 93–123; and Edward Rocklin, 'Marlowe as Experimental Dramatist: The Role of the Audience in *Jew of Malta*' in Kenneth Friedenreich, Roma Gill and Constance B. Kuriyama, eds., *'A Poet and a filthy Play-maker': New Essays on Christopher Marlowe*, 1988, pp. 129–42.
15 On the political usefulness of religious authority, see, e.g., *The Prince* XI; for Machiavelli's self-proclaimed lack of knowledge 'about profits or about losses' and his fitness only 'to reason about the state', see Albert O. Hirschman, *The Passions and the Interests*, 1977, p. 41.
16 N. W. Bawcutt argues that Marlowe shared his contemporaries' mixed acquaintance with Machiavellianism, compounded of reading Machiavelli as well as polemical accounts ('Machiavelli and Marlowe's *The Jew of Malta*', RenD 3 (1970), 3–49); compare Catherine Minshull, 'Marlowe's "Sound Machevill"', RenD 13 (1982), 35–53, who sees a contrast between the actual theories of Machiavelli (embodied in Ferneze) and popular distortions derived from Gentillet's account of Machiavellians as greedy and loving evil for its own sake. See also Bob Hodge, 'Marlowe, Marx, and Machiavelli: Reading into the Past' in David Aers et al., eds., *Literature, Language and Society in England 1580–1680*, 1981, pp. 1–22, who sees the play's plot contradicting the logic of the Prologue to suggest a sense of ideology as false consciousness in Barabas's confusions. Thomas Cartelli argues that Barabas adopts Machiavellian discourse and a spirit of 'moral abandon' rather than true Machiavellian principles (*Marlowe, Shakespeare and the Economy of Theatrical Experience*, 1991).

A more subtle contemporary dimension is provided by the play's engagement with the heteroglot socio-economic discourses of Elizabethan London. The frequent struggles involving London's population of 'strangers', struggles that had produced an atmosphere of crisis in the early 1590s, inform the play's language and action. Its treatment of the merchant stranger Barabas as well as its depiction of Maltese anti-Semitism may be seen in the context of anti-foreigner sentiments locally registered in public insurrection, Parliamentary debate, and the officially censored *Sir Thomas More* (1590–3?), with its depiction of English violence against London's foreign population.[17]

## Summary of the Plot

Introduced by a choric figure embodying murderous Machiavellian villainy, Barabas, the rich Jew of Malta, opens the play exulting in his enormous wealth, only to have it suddenly expropriated (along with his home) by the hypocritically Christian Maltese, who need his money to pay imperial tribute demanded by the Ottoman Turks. Barabas plots to regain his wealth by having his daughter pretend conversion to Christianity and thereby access gold he has hidden in his former house, now a nunnery; he also exploits her beauty to entrap fatally two sons of prominent Christians. Aided by a captured Turk, Ithamore, purchased from Malta's thriving slave market, Barabas manages to kill off the entire nunnery (including his daughter, who had alienated him by converting to Christianity) as well as two corrupt friars whom he entices with the prospect of his own lucrative conversion. Ithamore, seduced by a scheming prostitute, turns against Barabas and blackmails him to get money for his whore and her pimp. Barabas, ludicrously disguised as a French musician, kills all three with poisoned flowers, but is arrested for murder of his daughter's lovers. He escapes by feigning death as the Turks invade Malta, then betrays the island to the invaders, who install him as the new governor. However, he stupidly decides that he would be better off living under the former Christian Governor, whose son he had killed but whom he now entrusts with a plot to betray the Turks and regain power. Thinking thereby to earn the Governor's gratitude, Barabas blows up the Turkish troops with explosives, but the Governor catches him in the trap designed for the Turkish leaders, precipitating Barabas through a trapdoor and into a boiling pot where he dies cursing.

---

17  On anti-foreigner violence in the 1590s, see Ian W. Archer, *The Pursuit of Stability*, 1991, esp. pp. 131–48; Andrew Pettegree, *Foreign Protestant Communities* in *Sixteenth-Century London*, 1986. See also the appendix below, pp. 133–6.

# Staging

The stage history of *The Jew of Malta* before the twentieth century is sparse. The earliest sixteenth-century performances (1592–8), by various companies, were mostly at the Rose, where Edward Alleyn was the principal actor; evidence records frequent, well-attended performances, two physical circumstances (the cauldron and Barabas's 'artificiall . . . nose'), and we infer a third (a red wig and beard like that worn by Burbage as Shakespeare's Shylock).[18] One seventeenth-century production (by Queen Henrietta's company at the Cockpit or Phoenix and at Court) provides the single early text (1633). Evidence suggests other undocumented performances, perhaps in excerpted form, as well as German productions.[19] Before the twentieth century, the only English performance was Edmund Kean's 1818 production of Sampson Penley's adaptation 'founded on Marlowe's tragedy' but rendering Barabas a tragic victim of a corrupt society.

Penley substituted a prologue abjuring anti-Semitism, and added a scene detailing the love of Lodowick and Mathias for Abigail. He eliminated blasphemous self-comparison to Job, the farce of the poisoning of the nuns, the on-stage strangling of Bernardine, the poisoned flowers and the fatal cauldron. Barabas's catalogue of atrocities was treated as a rhetorical test of Ithamore, and Barabas was granted 'tragic solemnity'.[20] To my knowledge, there have been no clear theatrical successors to this approach, but recent productions have performed the play in tandem with Shakespeare's *Merchant of Venice*, sometimes even doubling the roles of Shylock and Barabas (Eric Porter, Stratford-upon-Avon, 1965; F. Murray Abraham, New York, 2007). Other productions, including that of the Classic Theatre, directed by Maurice Edwards (New York, 1987), that of the King Alfred's Performing Arts, directed by Stevie Simkin (Winchester, 1997) and that of the Almeida Theatre, directed by Michael Grandage (1999), have offset the play's negative treatment of Jews, not by avoiding the play's farcical elements, but by re-contextualizing them. Edwards set the play in the 1930s, gave the Maltese blackshirts and made Barabas a Jewish ham actor; Simkin set the play as if performed in 1939 Nazi-occupied Warsaw, offering the stage Jews a chance at dignity through subverting their textually-imposed stereotypes by overplaying or underplaying their expected 'roles'; Grandage cut Machiavell's Prologue and managed to suggest a Barabas needing love from Ithamore and

---

18  See Michael Hattaway, *Elizabethan Popular Theatre*, 1982, p. 81.
19  See Bawcutt's edition, p. 3.
20  See James L. Smith, '*The Jew of Malta* in the Theatre', in Brian Morris, ed., *Christopher Marlowe*, 1968, pp. 3-23, p. 9.

resisting the Nazi ovens.[21] The dominant note of modern productions has been exactly the farce Kean sought to avoid and that T. S. Eliot called the essence of the play.

The twentieth century's first American production was at Williams College, 1907; the first British production was the 1922 Phoenix Society performance in London (Smith, p. 4). That 1922 production was played as 'a monstrous farce' that emphasized the 'brutality' of Barabas and prompted audience laughter at the deaths of the lovers and the poisoning of the nuns (Smith, p. 11). Later productions did more to mix tonalities, but farce remains, even when satire is intended. One frequent satiric target is registered in the programme notes to a 1954 Reading University production, describing Barabas as transformed from a 'suffering and oppressed human figure into . . . [a] "prodigious caricature"' as an inept Machiavel who presents a 'satirically posed problem: Who then are the real villains of the story, the true followers of Machiavelli?' (Smith, p. 13). The speaker for the Prologue was significantly listed as '?', but many productions take Ferneze for the truer Machiavellian. The Marlowe Society production (Cambridge, 1975) directed by John Chapman, stood Machevill at Ferneze's elbow; the American Shakespeare Repertory production (1985), directed by Douglas Overtoom, doubled the parts; the Barry Kyle production (Stratford-upon-Avon, 1987, and later in London) concluded with Ferneze removing his wig to reveal himself the Machevill of the Prologue.[22] Still other productions take the play's comic energies as broader than such a narrowly defined target would allow.

Sick humour furnished inspiration for the 1964 productions of Peter Cheeseman (Victoria Theatre, Stoke-on-Trent) and Clifford Williams (RSC Aldwych Theatre; recast in Stratford 1965). Williams used speedy conjunctions and slapstick to emphasize contradictory elements and emotions: Barabas spits into the fatal porridge, Bernardine drops Abigail's body 'with a bump', Barabas and Ithamore shake hands behind Jacomo's back after framing him, Barabas performs as a Flamenco dancer while the deadly flowers circulate (Smith, pp. 15–18). Cheeseman wanted to release the audience from ordinary moral constraints by taking them into the world of the sick joke and to prompt them to understand Barabas as 'a cynical self-serving businessman' changed into a 'half-crazy gangster' by 'grasping Christian hypocrites' (Smith, pp. 19–20). This definition does

21  See Carolyn D. Williams (on Simkin), *CE* 55 (1999), 75–7; Peter J. Smith (on Grandage), *CE* 57 (2000), 126–8; and Lois Potter, 'Marlowe in Theatre and Film' in *The Cambridge Companion to Christopher Marlowe*, ed. Patrick Cheney, 2004, p. 271.

22  References, respectively, from *RORD* 18 (1975), 61; *RORD* 28 (1985), 165; and *TLS* (31 July 1987), p. 820.

not do justice to the production's misanthropic generality: the part of Machevill was acted by the same actor (the dramatist Alan Ayckborn) who played, not Ferneze, but the Spaniard Del Bosco and one of the Jews (Smith, p. 5). Similarly broad in its indictment of humanity, Williams's self-designated 'gangster epic' rendered Barabas as a professional wrong-doer among amateurs; one reviewer called him a 'clear sighted opportu-nist within a society that would act in the same way if it dared'.[23] Barabas exhibited a suave, well-groomed, confident demeanour, rich attire and a silver-tipped forelock, while opposing characters were weakened or dim-inished. Ferneze ended the play brandishing aloft a cross-shaped sword hilt, but the production cut some of his most aggressive lines (III.v.29–33; V.i. 1–2), subordinated him to both Del Bosco and Katherine (II.ii and III.ii) and had him cringe and back away from Barabas (V.v.20). Farce served a satire that aimed beyond Ferneze's Christian hypocrisy to indict 'dollar civilization' (Smith, p. 20–21).

In keeping with the play's broad targets and fluid use of space (e.g. in the frequent mid-scene location changes – I.ii from senate-house to out-side; II.iii from slave market to the door of Barabas's house; V.i from inside to outside Malta), modern productions have tended to the abstract. At its simplest, this has meant adding twentieth-century physical refer-ences, such as the 1984 Peter Benedict version that ended with Barabas in a microwave, or the 1985 American Shakespeare Repertory production that started with Barabas totalling figures on a pocket calculator and ended with his death in an electric chair wired to a time bomb intended to destroy everyone.[24] More spectacularly, non-English-speaking produc-tions have embraced expressionist resources to make their points. The 1976 Paris production, directed by Bernard Sobel, began with a dignified, cosmopolitan Barabas, who transforms himself in response to having his fortune extorted: the vengeful figure emerged from a trapdoor and put on an enormous cardboard nose, hunchback, limp, and claw-like hands.[25] Perhaps the most spectacular recent adaptation, André Werner's 2002 opera for the Munich Biennale, presented a non-linear, visually stun-ning confrontation between domination embodied in 'Machiavelli' and resistance arising from the players, the world and religion (Christianity, Judaism and Islam). Machiavelli initially controls the other actors, the action and the virtual architecture of rear-projecting screens; his gestures and movements command lighting that defines space and the reflective bodily surfaces of the other actors. However, eventually the characters

---

23 *The Times*, 2 October 1965.
24 *The Sunday Times*, 18 March 1984; *RORD* 28 (1985), 165.
25 See Potter, op. cit., p. 271.

revolt, removing their reflective garb, mocking Machiavelli, even control-
ling the virtual architecture themselves; ultimately, even the stage itself
rebels, subordinating the isolated Machiavelli to a stage densely filled
with the colours representing the three religions.[26]

## The Play

The 1633 quarto text of Marlowe's play is entitled *The Famous Tragedy of
the Rich Jew of Malta*, but by the time of its first modern revival (1818) it
was neither famous nor considered tragic.[27] One hundred years later, T.S.
Eliot also refused to call it a tragedy.[28] The issue was the nature and object
of the play's humour. Kean's revival struggled to create tragic dignity
from the play's representation of that transhistorical object of anti-
Semitism the 'rich Jew' who 'smiles to see how full his bags are crammed'.
The production added Sampson Penley's prologue, disclaiming intention
to 'cast opprobrium o'er the Hebrew name' and asserting moral universality: 'On every sect pernicious passions fall, / And vice and virtue reign
alike in all'.[29] The action was revised, especially in the last two acts, to give
Barabas greater dignity as a victim. Eliot's influential twentieth-century
assessment focused on these same final acts to conclude that the play was
no tragedy, not even a 'tragedy of blood', that popular Elizabethan revenge
genre, but 'farce' of 'terribly serious, even savage comic humour'. Subsequent criticism and staging have responded to the issues that concern
these pioneering instances of modern production and interpretation.

Kean's revision in the interests of Barabas's dignity and universality
and Eliot's redefinition of genre point to crucial features of Marlowe's
play. Humour is everywhere, and it is savage. Barabas delights in the deaths
of his victims:

> There is no music to a Christian's knell:
> How sweet the bells ring now the nuns are dead
> That sound at other times like tinkers' pans!     (IV.i. 1–3)

He invokes homey proverbs while committing mayhem:

---

26  See http://www.muenchenerbiennale.de/standard/en/archive/2002/marlowe-der-jude-
    von-malta/ ; for digital images, see http://www.artcom.de/index.php?lang=en&option=
    com_acprojects&id=29&Itemid=144&page=6; compare Stefanie Kuhn, 'Extended pres-
    ence: The instrumental(ised) body in André Werner's Marlowe: The Jew of Malta', *Inter-
    national Journal of Performance Arts and Digital Media* 2 (2007), 221–36.
27  See Smith, '*The Jew of Malta*', pp. 7–11, on Kean's performance.
28  Eliot's remarks are from 'Christopher Marlowe' in *Selected Essays*, 1964.
29  Smith, '*The Jew of Malta*', p. 7.

BERNARDINE
> What do you mean to strangle me?

ITHAMORE
> Yes, 'cause you use to confess.

BARABAS
> Blame not us but the proverb, 'Confess and be hanged'.
> Pull hard. (IV.i.144–7)

Even when he turns to high moral rhetoric, Barabas reminds the audience of the homicidal intentions beneath his words with strategic asides: 'As these have spoke so be it to their souls. / (I hope the poisoned flowers will work anon.)' (V.i.40–1). But Eliot calls the play's farcical violence 'serious'. What is perhaps most serious about the play is its insistent conceptual assault on the values and opinions of its audience.

The play's humour may be savage, but anthropologists have taught us that what appears 'savage' to one culture or group about another may be merely a product of cultural difference. The play differs from classical standards of high tragedy, whether defined by Aristotle, Sir Philip Sidney or Eliot, yet its relentless ironies make it much more than mere farce, sick comedy or crude racism. The ironies of a dramatic world where intention and strategy repeatedly come to unexpected, often catastrophic conclusions (e.g. Barabas's plans to conceal his wealth, to have his daughter feign conversion, to employ Ithamore, to profit from Ferneze's captivity, etc.) are compounded by reiteration of key terms (e.g. 'policy', 'profession'); by frequent and often wildly misappropriated allusions (e.g. Ithamore's ridiculous botch of Marlowe's 'Come live with me' or Barabas's twisted proverbs and bible verses); and by extensive, innovative use of asides. A clearer sense of what all these ingredients might add up to emerges if the play is evaluated not against some timeless definition of tragedy but in relation to the various tragic forms that it evokes, as well as in relation to institutions, concerns and discourses important to London of the 1590s – its theatre, religion and politics.

Marlowe's 'famous' play, arguably the most popular of the 1590s, repeatedly evokes alternative forms of tragedy, while remaining distinct from any of them. Friar Jacomo's exchange with Barabas raises the possibility of a tragedy resembling Sophocles' *Oedipus Rex*, with its arrogant Oedipus, who will not see his own errors, confronted by the literally blind prophet Teiresias, who perceives the source of Theban pollution all too clearly:

JACOMO
>Barabas, although thou art in misbelief,
>And wilt not see thine own afflictions,
>Yet let thy daughter be no longer blind.

BARABAS
>Blind, friar? I reck not thy persuasions.       (I.ii.349–52)

But neither Friar Jacomo, nor anyone else in Marlowe's play, is fit to assume, as Teiresias does, the voice of knowing rectitude. Instead, the official spokesmen of Christianity invoke pious platitudes while practicing violence and falsehood in eager pursuit of their own greed and lust.

If the tragic confrontation of wilful self-blindness with uncompromising knowledge is not appropriate as a model, neither is another Sophoclean form. Barabas and Ferneze briefly suggest a conflict of mutually exclusive 'rights' as embodied in the contests of Creon and Antigone in *Antigone* (translated by Marlowe's close associate Thomas Watson)[30]:

FERNEZE
>Content thee, Barabas, thou hast nought but right.

BARABAS
>Your extreme right does me exceeding wrong.       (I.ii.153–4)

Yet the 'right' claimed by the Maltese community is no less compromised than any other standard. The 'rights' at issue here amount to dubious international 'policy' and brutal domestic economy. The Maltese have stupidly acquiesced to a Turkish scheme allowing their debt to accumulate, thereby enabling the Turks to justify asserting their own right to imperial domination (I.i.180 ff), and the Maltese treat the Jews as a convenient source of revenue to make up for their own irresponsibility.

Closer in time and culture than classical models, Tudor narrative 'tragedies' (like *The Mirror for Magistrates*) concerned with the falls of princes appear echoed in Barabas's laments about time and mutability:

>The incertain pleasures of swift-footed time
>Have ta'en their flight, and left me in despair;
>And of my former riches rests no more
>But bare remembrance; like a soldier's scar,
>That has no further comfort for his maim.       (II.i.7–11)

---

30  Watson's translation is licensed in 1581.

But this lament is merely empty rhetoric, a brief moment in Barabas's hypocritical scheming to get his money back rather than a pathos-laden summation of life's tragedy as seen from death's threshold; within thirty lines Barabas is catching his money bags, thrown to him (as planned), by his complicitous daughter. Finally, Barabas also recalls Marlowe's own popular 'overreacher' tragedy of *Tamburlaine*.[31] Barabas – played by the same Edward Alleyn who had portrayed aspiring Tamburlaine – proclaims enormous global aspirations as a desire to 'inclose / Infinite riches in a little room' (I.i.36–7). Yet rhapsodic evocations of ambition quickly give way to multiple plots, schemes and poisonings. There are more apposite tragic models: Tudor homiletic tragedy, a form Marlowe experimented with in the innovative sequel to *Tamburlaine*, and revenge tragedy as developed in Thomas Kyd's enormously popular play, *The Spanish Tragedy*.

*The Jew of Malta* shares lines with *The Spanish Tragedy*, but the relationship extends beyond verbal borrowings to fundamental similarities and, ultimately, to some meaningful differences. Following Seneca, Kyd's play and Marlowe's open with a supernatural frame, dramatize violent revenge and indulge in extreme emotional rhetoric; but four innovative features of the Kydian dramatic form contribute to *The Jew of Malta*: its representation of social tensions, its deployment of multiple ironies, its interrelation of heroism and villainy and its humour.

Above all, Kyd's version of Senecan form is innovative in rendering tragedy concretely social. The action may be framed by Senecan ghosts and demons seeking their own bloody vengeance, but the protagonist and his victims are constructed within recognizable Elizabethan social tensions. Kyd's Hieronimo is arguably the first tragic protagonist to live and die amid the constraints of a middling condition.[32] He has to get up and go to work, despite his sufferings, in a world where status, money and education are significant factors. Such material-social considerations are absent from the Senecan inheritance. Nor does Seneca emphasize the ethical-metaphysical tensions that permeate Kyd's half-Christian dramatic universe. Despite its supernatural machinery, *The Spanish Tragedy* repeatedly suggests that Hieronimo the revenger must be evaluated against multiple ironies. These ironies are registered verbally, in allusions to the biblical injunction against revenge, or in the action, when a well-meaning bystander (Castile) and a sympathetic victim (Bel-Imperia) become collateral

---

31 Marlowe's works are discussed in these terms in Harry Levin's *The Overreacher: A Study of Christopher Marlowe*, 1952; recent studies have challenged the application of Levin's terms to *The Jew of Malta*.

32 On Kyd's middling protagonist, and the relation of Kyd and Marlowe, see James R. Siemon, 'Sporting Kyd', *ELR* 24 (1994), 553–82.

damage to Hieronimo's successful pursuit of revenge. Ironic intonations suggest that desire for vengeance impairs judgement: the ghost who opens the play as a victim seeking vengeance, becomes so enraptured by spectacular violence that his triumphant epilogue indiscriminately hails both the revenge upon his enemies and the destruction of his friends as 'spectacles to please my soul' (IV.v.12). Kyd's tragedy develops implicit similarities between villainy and heroism. The machinations of its cruel arch-villain, Lorenzo, are eventually mirrored by those of its increasingly cruel protagonist. Finally, potentially 'tragic' matters of life and death, justice and morality are laced with grotesque humour (Hieronimo eats the commoner's pleas for justice; an assassin is fatally tricked by an extended joke involving an empty box).

Both Hieronimo and Barabas belong to publicly detested categories, but by suffering obvious injustices stage Spaniard and stage Jew become potentially sympathetic characters. They begin their plays pursuing labours and aspirations defined by a 'profession', they display a critical awareness of international conflicts and alliances, and they come to neglect their professions in order to pursue revenge. Surmounting frustrations, they achieve remarkable success in their plots before falling in their moments of triumph. That said, obvious differences lie in Barabas's unabashed materialism, self-proclaimed conscienceless egocentrism, and eager affinity for violence. Barabas does not grow into bloodiness but professes an eagerly homicidal nature that predates the play or even a provocation (II.iii.173–200), and he expresses indifferent readiness to sacrifice Christian and Jew alike: 'let 'em combat, conquer, and kill all, / So they spare me, my daughter, and my wealth' (I.i.151–2). And, it is 'wealth' that he ultimately cares about, rather than some more acceptably universal value like Hieronimo's commitments to family and justice.[33] Rejecting the claims of 'conscience', 'faith' and 'principality', Barabas interprets biblical 'blessings promised to the Jews' as material 'plenty'.

When he does suffer losses – of money, property, his daughter's heart or her religious allegiance – Barabas responds not proportionately but with murder, even mass murder. To him every injury is a capital offence. Furthermore, the very first time we are invited to sympathize with him in his miseries, Barabas does something Hieronimo never does: he deceives us, and mocks us to boot, as he laughs at his on-stage sympathizers:

---

33 Barabas echoes the self-definition of Envy – 'I am Envy . . . O that there would come a famine through all the world, that all might die, and I live alone' (*Dr Faustus* V. 303–7) – in his own proclamation – 'For so I live, perish may all the world' (V. v. 10); see Erich Segal, 'Marlowe's *Schadenfreude*: Barabas as Comic Hero', in Harry Levin, ed., *Veins of Humor*, 1972, pp. 69–92 (p. 84).

> See the simplicity of these base slaves,
> Who for the villains have no wit themselves,
> Think me to be a senseless lump of clay
> That will with every water wash to dirt:
> No, Barabas is born to better chance,
> And framed of finer mould than common men,
> That measure nought but by the present time.
> A reaching thought will search his deepest wits,
> And cast with cunning for the time to come:
> For evils are apt to happen every day.                    (I.ii.216–25)

Like 'common men', we may have been cheated into 'misplaced sympathy'[34], but after this moment it is unlikely we will ever 'trust Barabas . . . [or] pity him again'.[35] This disillusionment sets up the very next moment of the play when we are invited to laugh at him – not with him – as his self-proclaimed superiority of wit and foresight, his 'reaching thought', is thwarted by Governor Ferneze's seizure of his treasure. This time his lamentation is unfeigned and unpitied (I.ii.258–65).

The ironic rhythm of boastful contrivance, limited success and subsequent laughable difficulty recalls an old theatrical standby. Barabas's final, fatal boast proclaims his descent from the braggart villains and vices of earlier drama – 'Now tell me, worldlings, underneath the sun, / If greater falsehood ever has been done' (V.v.49–50) – just before he drops into a boiling 'cauldron' of his own making.[36] The archaic dramaturgy of Tudor hybrid homiletic drama seems confirmed by Ferneze's concluding epitaph thanking 'heaven' for safeguarding the Christian community against Barabas's 'unhallowed deeds'. Does the play endorse this conclusion, pronounced by one who has appropriated the evildoer's own treacherous machinery while abusing his religion and race?

*The Jew of Malta* is not Marlowe's first play to represent cross-cultural antagonists caught in their own hypocritical devices amid invocations of

34  Bevington, *Mankind to Marlowe*, p. 225.
35  Robert C. Jones, *Engagement with Knavery: Point of View in Richard III, The Jew of Malta, Volpone and The Revenger's Tragedy*, 1986; contrast Jones's sense of audience alienation with Stephen Greenblatt's assertions of identification with Barabas ('Marlowe, Marx, and Anti-Semitism' in *Learning to Curse: Essays in Early Modern Culture*, 1990, pp. 40–58, (esp. pp. 50–1)); James L Simmons ('Elizabethan Stage Practice and Marlowe's *Jew of Malta*', *RenD* 4 (1971), 93–104, esp. pp. 103–4); and J. B. Steane (*Marlowe: A Critical Study*, 1974). esp. p. 172).
36  On the play's relation to morality drama and its Vice figures, see Bernard Spivack, *Shakespeare and the Allegory of Evil*, 1958, esp. pp. 346–55. Spivack notes this speech's 'didactic and demonstrative principle, its ironic inversion of the homiletic point, its rallying impeachment of the audience, its celebration of deceit' (p. 351). Compare Lunney, *Marlowe and the Popular Tradition*, on the play's exploitation of this tradition.

divine Providence. The Christians of *Tamburlaine II* suspect that their allies, the 'heathenish Turks and pagans' (II.i.6), will betray them, so they preemptively violate their sworn oaths of alliance and, ultimately, suffer the consequences. The key terms in their fatal mistake are religious 'profession' and worldly 'policy'.[37] First, the Christians argue that Muslims are 'infidels' and thus not to be trusted; for good measure, they also claim that keeping a promise with the Muslims would violate 'necessary policy', a widely, if uneasily, recognized demand of statecraft, which, adapting Machiavelli, posited self-interest as a universal rule of political conduct. Furthermore, the Christians also argue that keeping such an oath is actually 'sinful' because circumstances have provided a Providential 'opportunity' to act on God's behalf against 'blasphemous paganism'. These arguments are all recognizably Elizabethan; however, the play renders them suspect.[38] Any Protestant could recognize this situation, in which policy and opportunity trump profession and oath, as recalling notorious instances of Roman Catholic treachery; any churchgoer might detect the supporting biblical precedents to be misappropriated for selfish uses.[39]

Both *Tamburlaine II* and *The Jew of Malta* represent European Christianity encountering a non-Christian Other, and both reveal religious 'profession' to be entwined with worldly 'policy'. The first lines of the Prologue – spoken by the embodiment of policy, the spirit of Niccolò Machiavelli – emphasize the politics of religious vocation. Throughout the play, the word 'policy' is reiterated thirteen times (against six instances in all of Marlowe's other works) often in tandem with 'profession' (see e.g. I.ii.161–2)[40]. Furthermore, there are important similarities

---

37 On 'policy', see N.W. Bawcutt, '"Policy", Machiavellianism, and the Earlier Tudor Drama', *ELR* 1 (1971), 195–209; also Howard S. Babb, 'Policy in Marlowe's *Jew of Malta*', *ELH* 24 (1957), 85–94.

38 During the siege of Malta in 1565 prayers are appointed beseeching God to defend the island against 'the rage and violence of Infidels, who, by all tyranny and cruelty labour utterly to root out not only true Religion, but also the very name and memory of Christ our only Saviour, and all Christianity' (Hunter, 229). Queen Elizabeth refers to the Turks in 1596 as 'the common enemy of Christ' (G.B. Harrison, ed., *The Letters of Queen Elizabeth*, 1935, p. 243). But England and France had ties and offered aid to the Ottomans, enlisting the Sultan as a counterweight to Habsburg power (see Carl Max Kortepeter, *Ottoman Imperialism During the Reformation: Europe and the Caucasus*, 1972, pp. 1–2). For an excellent account of the play within the dynamics of imperialism, see Emily C. Bartels, *Spectacles of Strangeness: Imperialism, Alienation and Marlowe*, 1993.

39 On the relationships of the Sigismund-Orcanes episodes of *Tamburlaine II* to notorious cases of Catholic oath breaking, see Roy W. Battenhouse, 'Protestant Apologetics and the Subplot of 2 *Tamburlaine*', *ELR* 3 (1973), 30–43. For casuistry as a divisive issue, see Edmund Leites, ed., *Conscience and Casuistry in Early Modern Europe*, 1988.

40 Word frequency counts from Bawcutt, p. 54.

in dramatic moralizing that link *The Jew of Malta* with the Sigismund episodes of *Tamburlaine II*. Mortal defeat leads the Christian forces to recognize that what they had called 'necessary policy' was actually 'sin', while the Muslims, for their part, embrace Christ as well as Mohammed, proclaiming an ecumenical universalism that judges all humanity by the same standards: 'Can there be such deceit in Christians, / Or treason in the fleshly heart of man, / Whose shape is figure of the highest God?' (II.ii.36–8). By giving the moral to the Muslims, Marlowe ensures there is no missing its point: 'deceit' is bad no matter how it may be supported by discourses of politic self-interest, ethno-centrism or religious prejudice – even one's own. But the clear representation of this humanist moral universal in *Tamburlaine II* differs greatly from Marlowe's complicated presentation of the expropriation of Barabas's wealth and the death of his daughter, Abigail.

Abigail expresses justifiable pity for her father's suffering at the hands of the Christians, undertakes to redress his 'wrongs', becomes enmeshed in his 'policy', suffers mortal consequences and piously repents. Her final self-accounting constitutes tragic *anagnoresis* or recognition in Christian terms:

> I was chained to follies of the world:
> But now experience, purchasèd with grief,
> Has made me see the difference of things.
> My sinful soul, alas, hath paced too long
> The fatal labyrinth of misbelief,
> Far from the Son that gives eternal life.          (III.iii.60–5)

Painful 'experience' has clarified a 'difference' between worldly illusion and the certainty of the Christian promise of eternal life. This is orthodox enough, but that this edifying Christian end should come to this character, and within its specific circumstances, is deeply ironic. The 'difference' that has prompted Abigail's recognition is not merely a metaphysical difference between worldly folly and heavenly certainties, but a prejudicial distinction between races and religions. Abigail, who is herself a Jew, who alone among the play's characters expresses pity, and who has loved both a Jewish father and Christian fiancé, proclaims: 'I perceive there is no love on earth, / Pity in Jews, nor piety in Turks' (III.iii.47–8). That she should betray her own virtues in such an expression suggests a confusion that goes beyond the convert's passion; but her misrecognitions further prompt her to commit herself to Malta's grossly hypocritical friars, as if they embodied Christian virtues. Just in case one might miss the irony of her misperception, her dying profession, imploring Friar Bernardine to 'witness that I die a Christian', is answered by his leering mockery of love, pity and piety: 'Ay, and a virgin too, that grieves me most' (III.vi.41).

Why does the play make professed Christians look so bad? Is it because they are all 'Catholic' and 'foreign' and hence fair game for Elizabethan sectarian mockery? Or is this an attempt at even-handedness (like Kean's prologue)? The play does suggest a universal economic determinism is at work across all lines of religion and nation. The Turkish Bashaw presumes that 'all the world' is driven by 'Desire of gold' (III.v.3–4). Barabas claims none to be 'honoured now but for his wealth' (I.i.112), and statecraft, religion, sex and even poetry are treated as economic pursuits. The play's market (II.iii) wonderfully suggests a world where all relationships are subject to material definition by bringing together Christian slaving (with 'every one's price written on his back'), Lodowick's negotiating the 'price' of Abigail's love, Katherine's evaluating which slave is 'comeliest' for her money and Barabas's choice to purchase lean Ithamore because his physique promises reduced expense for upkeep. Yet to insist on any such single standard of evaluation seems inadequate to account for a play in which multiple moral issues are repeatedly, in T. W. Craik's phrase, 'ironically touched upon and left'.[41] After all, in this very scene, Barabas jauntily dismisses his costly defrauding with 'I have wealth enough', and chooses to pursue the revenge that – often to his economic cost – dominates his attention.

*The Jew of Malta* is innovative not because it depicts a world driven by any single viciousness epitomized in any single Vice figure – older hybrid morality plays like Preston's *Cambyses* had done that – or because its characters individually violate clear-cut standards of ethical behaviour, but because their practices and perceptions are so often complicated, as is Abigail's own conversion, by distorted misrecognitions that are formed, articulated and supported socially. The same 'vice and virtue' do not 'reign alike in all'; instead vices and virtues, like the mistakes that accompany them, are made specific to institutions and situations. The play's pervasive ironies constantly remind one of this fact. However much Jew, Turk and Christian resemble one another and, ultimately, Barabas in their wrongs, pretences and miscalculations, they are differentiated according to occupation or role. As an imperial lord, Calymath assumes that it is 'more kingly to obtain by peace / Than to enforce conditions by constraint'

---

41  See Craik's edition, p. xiv; compare Constance Brown Kuriyama, *Hammer or Anvil: Psychological Patterns in Christopher Marlowe's Plays*, 1980, on Malta and 'universal lust for self-gratification' (p. 171).

(I.ii.25–6), trusts in the spying that his 'kingly' delay necessitates, and loses everything. As governor of Malta, Ferneze lets tribute payments lapse (I.ii), politically reinterprets his mistake as 'Honour[able]' resistance to Turkish tyranny in order to gain Spanish support (II.ii) and suffers all but total defeat and humiliation. As a victorious admiral, Del Bosco seeks to sell Turks in Malta, cleverly recasts his marketing problems as defence of the honour of 'Christendom' (II.ii), but fails to produce sufficient Spanish might to match the Turks. As spiritual confessor, Friar Bernardine cleverly violates 'canon law' enjoining confessional sanctity (III.vi) to blackmail Barabas, but stupidly trusts a confession extorted from Barabas (IV.i) and is killed. Falsifying his professed love for Mathias, Lodowick nevertheless believes he can credit Barabas's and Abigail's own feigned professions of love (II.iii) and pays with his life. These violations and miscalculations are defined by social categories – king, governor, admiral, priest, lover – as are the equally self-defeating duplicities of the play's courtesan, pickpocket and slave. Barabas epitomizes the relation of specific vices to specific roles in his over-the-top curriculum vitae: he studied medicine to produce 'dead men's knells', became an engineer to slay 'friend and enemy', and practiced finance to pursue 'extorting, cozening, forfeiting, / And tricks belonging unto brokery' (II.iii. 180–200). Ironically, however, dull-witted Ithamore will prove smart enough to give the cunning arch-misanthrope of all trades a very difficult time.

Social definitions are obviously important whenever Barabas is involved. He takes himself for an isolato, embracing his outcast status as a loner, proclaiming '*Ego mihimet sum semper proximus*' (I.i.188), but cannot escape contradictory positions: positively the *rich* Jew of Malta and negatively the rich *Jew* of Malta, though he is never really 'of' Malta to the Maltese, either, and the Jews are wrong to take him for theirs.[42] Barabas serves to focus attention on the diverse ways ethnic and religious identity inflect behaviour, business practices, communal affiliation, family affection, physical demeanour, wealth and cleverness. Sometimes his own identity appears compounded of his calculated anticipations of the prejudices of others. Thus, he excuses his daughter's weeping as 'the Hebrews' guise, / That maidens new betrothed should weep a while' (II.iii.324–5). Or, he produces a confession befitting Christian commonplaces concerning 'Jewish' partisan zealotry, pitilessness, greed, usury, wealth and hypocrisy:

---

42  For anti-Semitic discourse generally, compare note 11 above; for Jewishness as symbolic of fa ings in Christianity, see Alan C. Dessen, 'The Elizabethan Stage Jew and Christian Example: Gerontus, Barabas, and Shylock', *MLQ* 35 (1974), 231–45; compare Hunter; Kocher, *Christopher Marlowe*; and Katz, *Philo-Semitism* (p. 162).

I have been zealous in the Jewish faith,
Hard-hearted to the poor, a covetous wretch,
That would for lucre's sake have sold my soul.
A hundred for a hundred I have ta'en;
And now for store of wealth may I compare
With all the Jews in Malta; but what is wealth?
I am a Jew, and therefore am I lost.                    (IV.i.51–7)

Other moments are not so simply calculated. The very sight of Lodowick prompts visceral revulsion, his shaven face – like 'a hog's cheek new singed' (II.iii.42) – epitomizing Christian differences of diet and countenance. He also sometimes rejoices in performing the stereotyped 'Jew':

We Jews can fawn like spaniels when we please;
And when we grin we bite, yet are our looks
As innocent and harmless as a lamb's.
I learned in Florence how to kiss my hand,
Heave up my shoulders when they call me dog,
And duck as low as any bare-foot friar,
Hoping to see them starve upon a stall,
Or else be gathered for in our synagogue;
That when the offering-basin comes to me,
Even for charity I may spit into't.                     (II.iii.20–9)

In a related vein, he advises Abigail to deceive Lodowick 'like a cunning Jew' (II.iii.234). What should we make of a play that gives lines like these to a Jewish character? The answer may better follow a consideration of the expropriation of Barabas's wealth.

The Maltese officials, like Abigail, are hostile to Jews, but, unlike her, they purposely invoke impeccable early modern authority rather than confused personal experience to ground their hostility. Echoing polemic ultimately derived from Matthew 32, Ferneze calls Jews 'infidels . . . accursed in the sight of heaven' for the guilt which is attributed to them collectively in accounts of the crucifixion of Christ. Thus, the seizure of Barabas's wealth is justified with a reminder of the divinely ordained punishment appropriate for this 'inherent' guilt:

If your first curse fall heavy on thy head,
And make thee poor and scorned of all the world,
'Tis not our fault, but thy inherent sin.   (I.ii.108–10)

Furthermore, official Malta defines its own political misfortune in terms familiar to Elizabethan state discourse: the tribute demanded by the Turks is called a Providential punishment for the 'sin' of religious toleration. Ferneze tells the Jews, it is 'through our sufferance of your hateful lives . . . These taxes and afflictions are befallen' (I.ii.63–5).[43]

However orthodox, the religiously sanctioned extortion of Jewish wealth is framed by lines that reiterate suspicions about religious profession.[44] Barabas warns us to beware Christian 'malice, falsehood, and excessive pride' unfitting their 'profession' (I.i.116–17). During the seizure, he demands of the Christians, 'Bring you scripture to confirm your wrongs?' (I.ii.111); and afterwards he accurately assesses their tactics: 'policy? that's their profession, / And not simplicity, as they suggest' (I.ii.161–2). Furthermore, the play grants its victimized Jew ethically powerful and biblically-derived defenses. Barabas counters the biblically-derived imputation of racial guilt with an assertion of individual moral responsibility that echoes Proverbs 10 ('The treasures of wickednes profite nothing: but righteousness delivereth from death'):

> But say the tribe that I descended of
> Were all in general cast away for sin,
> Shall I be tried by their transgression?
> The man that dealeth righteously shall live:
> And which of you can charge me otherwise? (I.ii.114–18)

Finally, Christian assertions are riddled with their own ironic elements. From Caiaphas's justification of the persecution of Christ comes Ferneze's claim 'better one want for a common good, / Than many perish for a private man' (I.ii.99–100; cf. John 11:50); and Pilate's self-exculpation provides Ferneze's image of clean hands, 'Barabas, to stain our hands with blood / Is far from us and our profession' (I.ii.145–6; cf. Matthew 27:24).[45] Barabas may be more like the AntiChrist, than like Christ, but

---

43 Compare the charges of 1601 against Sir Christopher Blunt, for seeking 'toleration of religion' (William Cobbett, *Complete Collection of State Trials*, 1809, vol. 1, pp. 1421–2). Alexander Ross claims that 'Diversity of *Religions* beget envy, malice, seditions, factions, rebellions, contempt of Superiours, treacheries, innovations, disobedience, and many more mischiefs, which pull down the heavy judgements of God upon that State or Kingdom, where contrary *Religions* are allowed' (*[Pansebeia] Or, A View of all Religions in the World*, 4th ed., 1664, p. 506).

44 On treating Jews as 'indirect tax-collectors', see Pollins, *Economic History*, p. 19; for similar treatment of Protestant 'strangers' see Pettegree, *Foreign Protestant Communities*, p. 294.

45 On the notoriety of John 11:50 and its uses in arguments about the mysteries of state, see Peter S. Donaldson, *Machiavelli and Mystery of State*, 1988, p. 175.

the words of the professed Christians insistently echo the persecutors of Christ.[46] The hypocrisy of preaching against wealth while expropriating wealth appears registered even in the form of Ferneze's utterances. 'Excess of wealth is cause of covetousness: /And covetousness, oh 'tis a monstrous sin' (I.ii.124–5), he says, but the interjected 'oh' makes his pious maxim sound suspiciously unctuous. Barabas's response – 'Ay, but theft is worse: tush, take not from me then' (126) – counterpunches metrically, interjection for interjection.

Thus far, the treatment of conflict between Jew and Christian recalls the ethical critique of Christian worldly practice in *Tamburlaine II*. But the play might also remind its Elizabethan audience of contemporary extra-theatrical conflicts. If London had no openly practicing Jews, it had its own marginal groups, and among them was one community thought to share occupations and values, if not religion, with Jews: the merchant 'strangers'.[47] These resident Protestants, mainly from France and the Netherlands, aroused sometimes violent animosities that were articulated in terms, economic, religious, and behavioural, that echo the language of historical anti-Semitism.[48]

Like Barabas himself, the Stranger is deemed a 'Machiavellian' monster comprised of attitudes, practices and associations that infect every level and aspect of society. Strangers are reputed both to be subservient to powers of state and to harbour revolutionary desires, to be both hypocritical and religiously fanatical, to spy for domestic authorities and to be complicit with foreign enemies. They are said to forge links with the volatile lower orders as well as dubious ties with the nobility; they are guilty both of labourless exploitation as usurers and of working too much in ambitious pursuit of multiple trades. These charges are most interesting in two articulations involving politics, economics and spectacle. The same merchant figure denounced in a standard Tudor litany of disapproved economic practices, including usury, engrossing, forestalling and unauthorized retailing, is also damned in terms political and antitheatrical: as a 'Machiavellian', who 'Undoeth thowsands' with 'his horrible showes'.

Historical explanations partially account for the charges of Machiavellianism. Since Gentillet, France had been commonly associated with Machiavellian politics, and Huguenot resistance to authority had made

---

46  On the Antichrist figure and *Jew of Malta*, see John Parker, *The Aesthetics of Antichrist: From Medieval Drama to Marlowe*, 2007, pp. 193–209.

47  See Pettegree, *Foreign Protestant Communities*; also Archer, *The Pursuit of Stability*, esp. pp. 131–48.

48  See Appendix below (pp. 133–6) for the relevant discourse.

them suspect, despite their Protestant credentials.[49] Whatever their distance from exalted statecraft, Continental immigrants might be understandably associated with the popular notion of Machiavelli as legitimating amoral self-interest.[50] There was also a felt distrust of the dimly understood, but much denounced, practices and values of emergent capitalism.[51]

Among all the charges against strangers that might resonate with the person and career of Barabas, none seems to me so potentially interesting for the play as the charge concerning 'horrible showes'. The parts of *The Jew of Malta* that have most troubled the critics, after all, have been, as they are in *Doctor Faustus*, those episodes in which the play's initial tragic impetus toward a 'moral' conclusion is delayed by seemingly gratuitous diversions: the 'delud[ing]' of the amorous Lodowick with shows of love (II.iii); the 'cunningly performed' (II.iii.366) duel that entraps the lovers and prompts Ithamore to praise its being 'So neatly plotted, and so well performed' (III.iii.2); Barabas's 'dissemble[d]' conversion (IV.i.47); the framing of Friar Jacomo with the artfully posed corpse of Friar Bernardine (IV.i); Barabas's performance in 'disguise' (IV.iii.65) as a French musician bearing poisoned flowers (IV.iv); and his fake death (V.i). Perhaps it is something analogous to this substitution of manner for matter, of diverting contrivance for solid substance, of 'gawds' for 'goods', of Mephistophilis' 'shows' for true omniscience, that renders the strangers' advanced marketing practices, and even their more highly wrought goods, suspect.[52]

Barabas himself constantly seeks to anticipate the demands of his Maltese consumers. Despite brilliant successes, especially his provision of

49 See J.H.M. Salmon, *The French Religious Wars in English Political Thought*, 1959. In Marlowe's youth, Canterbury was a centre of violent religious factionalism and of Huguenot immigration (Peter Clark, 'Josias Nicholls and Religious Radicalism, 1553–1639', *Journal of Ecclesiastical History* 28 (1977), 133–50).

50 On the stage Machiavel as a self-interested person rather than a political exponent, see Katherine Eisamon Maus, *Inwardness and Theater in the English Renaissance*, 1995.

51 See Marx's chapters on 'Primitive Accumulation' and on English agricultural expropriation in vol. 2 of *Capital*, 1981, and chapters 20 and 36 of vol. 3, in which the 'twin brothers' – merchant capital and usurer's capital – are analysed as forms of capital preceding capitalist modes of production. Compare the early modern 'reconceptualization of economic life' described in Joyce Oldham Appleby, *Economic Thought and Ideology in Seventeenth-century England*, 1978.

52 On the market for such goods, see Joan Thirsk, *Economic Policy and Projects: The Development of a Consumer Society in Early Modern England*, 1978. For marketing and theatre-like deception, compare the 1552 complaint: 'Could merchants, without lies, false making their wares, and selling them by a crooked light, to deceive the chapman in the thread or colour, grow so soon rich and to a baron's possessions, and make all their posterity gentlemen?' (in Gamini Salgado, ed., *Cony Catchers and Bawdy Baskets*,1972, p. 43). For Marlowe's relation to anti-theatricalism, see Debra Belt, 'Anti-Theatricalism and Rhetoric in Marlowe's *Edward II*', *ELR* 21 (1991), 134–65.

confessions to fulfill the Friars' demands to reveal himself as 'a wicked Jew' (IV.i.24), his remarkably frequent asides reveal virtually every utterance to be a strategic distortion. He attempts, in Machevill's phrase, to 'guard' his true values, keeping them from his tongue so he may market 'himself' successfully. Even his 'true' confessions to the Friars are strategic – telling the truth with as much attention to situation as if it were a lie.[53] Thus, it is appropriate that Barabas proclaims the moral equivalence and strategic superiority of conscious individual hypocrisy to unthinking, blind entrapment in communal social rituals:

> As good dissemble that thou never mean'st
> As first mean truth and then dissemble it;
> A counterfeit profession is better
> Than unseen hypocrisy.                    (I.ii.290–3)

Yet Barabas really does not do all that well in turning counterfeit shows of agreement or compliance to use in 'Making a profit of . . . policy' (V.ii.112). The 'business' of statecraft (V.ii.110) depends, as does the 'policy' of economic life, on forces beyond the power of the isolated individual strategist, no matter how demonic in energy, ruthless in analysis or proficient in counterfeiting. Over and over again, self-serving schemes come to 'unseen' conclusions owing to overlapping and interlocking circumstances of an emotional, economic, religious and political nature. One might call the effects of this larger field of conditions, alliances and discourses the work of 'heaven', as does Ferneze in the play's final line, but its pitiless workings suggest this name might be a misrecognition of something else.

That something else might be called by names that Ferneze rejects: 'fate' or 'fortune', the one pertaining to the causality of classical tragedy and the other to the perverse chance which Machiavelli's agents must contend with in their pursuit of power and glory. Yet, the crucial role played by the play's strategists themselves in their own undoing might lead one to wonder if Marlowe's play suggests through its paradoxes an intellectual space for what would later be identified as ideology, the internalization of the 'unseen' social determinants of discourse and epistemology.[54] The self-deception that brings down Barabas resembles that which levels Faustus, Marlowe's other protagonist who is also notably too

---

53  Compare Emily Bartels, *Spectacles of Strangeness*, on Barabas 'strategically play[ing] the Jew'; contrast David H. Thurn on the reduction of Barabas to 'manifest Jew' in 'Economic and Ideological Exchange in Marlowe's *Jew of Malta*', *TJ* 46 (1994), pp. 157–70.

54  Bob Hodge usefully analyzes ideology in the play (see note 16 above).

smart, and not smart enough, for his own good. Like Machevill, both Barabas and Faustus condescend to 'petty wits' who rest content within social limitations instead of pursuing the independence promised by policy or magic. Yet neither can escape values assumed by the social order they reject, Faustus oddly affirming 'resolut[ion]' in 'manly fortitude' (V.6; III.86) over the evidence of his own senses, Barabas stupidly choosing 'profit' over 'authority' (V.ii.27–46), under the orthodox, but patently illusory, assumption that 'peaceful rule [with] Christians kings' (I.i.133) will prove better for him than the continuation of a state of war.

This drama of half-swallowed asides and uncompleted sentences, of grotesquely hypocritical rhetoric, of grossly hyperbolic violence, of pervasive, cynical economic motivation and of religious and ethnic resentments has no clear successors in Marlowe's own brief canon. The twenty-first century needs no lessons in hatred and prejudice, to be sure, nor any help from sensational drama to foster brutality and cynicism. But in a post-modern world grown increasingly global in economics and in lived experience, one may regret the lack of further Marlovian exploration in the social vein opened by *The Jew of Malta*.[55] The play's potential to disturb the unspoken 'doxa' of its own social order suggests no small risk for its first producers.[56] The risk of modern theatrical production is that, deprived of its Elizabethan contexts and thereby of many of its multiple ironies, the play's nightmare representation of anti-Semitism's hated object will constitute encouragement of prejudice. This danger is a factor to be reckoned with in the play's stage history.

## The Text

Although *The Jew of Malta* was entered in the Stationers' Register for 17 May 1594, the only early text for it is the 1633 quarto published by Nicholas Vavasour and printed in the shop of John Beale (I.B.). I have used the Bodleian Library copy (shelf mark Mal. 172 [2]), consulting as well copies from the British Library (shelf mark 82.c.22 [5]) and the Houghton Library (shelf mark 14416.35.15). I have compared modern editions of N.W. Bawcutt (The Revels Plays, 1978), H.S. Bennett (*The Jew of Malta and The Massacre at Paris*, 1931), Fredson Bowers (*The Complete*

55 On transnationalism and tribalism, see John F. Stack, ed., *Ethnic Identities in a Transnational World*, 1981, esp. pp. 18–36; compare Fredric Jameson on postmodern group consciousness (*Postmodernism or, the Cultural Logic of Late Capitalism*, 1991, esp. pp. 346–8).
56 'Doxa' is Pierre Bourdieu's term for an 'undisputed, pre-reflexive, naïve, native compliance with the fundamental presuppositions' of a culture or one of its sub-fields; its unspoken 'unanimity effect' results from that which literally goes without saying (*The Logic of Practice*, 1990, p. 68).

*Works of Christopher Marlowe*, 1981), T.W. Craik (New Mermaids, 1966), R.A. Fraser (*Drama of the English Renaissance*, 1976), J.B. Steane (*The Complete Plays of Christopher Marlowe*, 1969), R.W. Van Fossen (Regents Renaissance Drama, 1964), and Mark Thornton Burnett, *The Complete Plays of Christopher Marlowe* (Everyman Library, 1999).

On the basis of perceived disunity of style and tone, it has been argued that the quarto reflects revision, probably by Thomas Heywood; but studies of vocabulary, spelling, metre and dramaturgy have generally supported the opinion that the quarto derives from a Marlovian original.[57] Despite numerous trivial printing errors, the quarto text presents few difficulties. Its inconsistency in speech prefixes (e.g. Barabas is *Iew* in 1.i. and elsewhere *Bar.*; Friar Jacomo is *1 Fry.* except in IV.i., where he is *Ioco.*) and names (e.g. Ithamore is usually Ithimore, sometimes Ithimer), and its frequent omission of entries, exits and other stage directions, have suggested to some that the text is derived from a relatively clean copy of authorial 'foul papers' rather than from theatrical prompt copy.

The quarto text is divided into acts; scenes have been added for the present edition. Spelling has been modernized, but, mindful of Ethel Seaton's observations on the potential implications of punctuation in other Marlovian texts – especially the frequently used colon – I have retained early punctuation wherever it did not seem to present serious difficulty.[58] In many instances the printers appear to have relined prose as verse (e.g. IV.ii.40–3; V.i.31–2). Changes in lineation have been noted. The exceptionally extensive use of asides presents challenges, since the precise beginning and end points are sometimes unclear (e.g. I.i.172); the quarto occasionally employs italics with the direction 'aside' to mark the extent of the aside (e.g. II.iii.82), and such passages are noted. This edition marks asides throughout with parentheses; when characters speak aside with one another, one set of parentheses encloses the entire conversation (e.g. IV.iv.23–4); otherwise separate parentheses are employed for each aside. Editorial additions, except those noted in the footnotes, appear in square brackets. The abbreviation 'ed.' refers to emendation by any editor.

57  See Bawcutt, pp. 39–46.
58  Ethel Seaton, 'Marlowe's Map', *Essays and Studies 10* (1924), 31–2.

# FURTHER READING

Bartels, Emily C., ed., *Critical Essays on Christopher Marlowe*, 1997

Bartels, Emily C., 'Malta, the Jew, and the Fictions of Difference: Colonialist Discourse in Marlowe's *The Jew of Malta*', *ELR* 20 (1990), 1–16

————, *Spectacles of Strangeness: Imperialism, Alienation and Marlowe*, 1993

Bawcutt, N.W., 'Machiavelli and Marlowe's *The Jew of Malta*', *RenD* n.s. 3 (1970), 3–49

Berek, Peter, 'The Jew as Renaissance Man', *Renaissance Quarterly*, 51 (1998), 128–162

Bevington, David, *From Mankind to Marlowe*, 1962

Cartelli, Thomas, *Marlowe, Shakespeare and the Economy of Theatrical Experience*, 1991

Cheney, Patrick, *Marlowe's Counterfeit Profession: Ovid, Spenser, Counternationhood*, 1997

Cheney, Patrick, ed., *The Cambridge Companion to Christopher Marlowe*, 2004

Deats, Sara Munson and Lisa S. Starks, '"So Neatly Plotted, and So Well Perform'd": Villain as Playwright in Marlowe's *The Jew of Malta*', *TJ* 44 (1992), 375–89

Dessen, Alan C., 'The Elizabethan Stage Jew and Christian Example: Gerontus, Barabas, and Shylock', *MLQ* 35 (1974), 231–45

Downie, J.A. and J.T. Parnell, eds., *Constructing Christopher Marlowe*, 2000

Friedenreich, Kenneth, Roma Gill and Constance B. Kuriyama, *'A Poet and a filthy Play-maker': New Essays on Christopher Marlowe*, 1988

Goldberg, Dena, 'Sacrifice in Marlowe's *The Jew of Malta*', *SEL* 32 (1992), 233–45

Grantley, Darryll and Peter Roberts, eds., *Christopher Marlowe and English Renaissance Culture*, 1996

Greenblatt, Stephen, 'Marlowe, Marx, and Anti-Semitism, in *Learning to Curse: Essays in Early Modern Culture*, 1990

Healey, Thomas, *Christopher Marlowe*, 1994

Hodge, Bob, 'Marlowe, Max, and Machiavelli; Reading into the Past', in David Aers et al., eds, *Literature, Language and Society in England, 1580–1680*, 1981

Hunter, G. K., 'The Theology of Marlowe's *The Jew of Malta*', *JWCI* 27 (1964), 211–40

Jones, Robert C., *Engagement with Knavery: Point of View in Richard III, The Jew of Malta, Volpone and The Revenger's Tragedy*, 1986

Kocher, Paul H., *Christopher Marlowe: A Study of His Thought, Learning and Character*, 1946

Levin, Harry, *The Overreacher: A Study of Christopher Marlowe*, 1952

Lunney, Ruth, *Marlowe and the Popular Tradition: Innovation in the English Drama before 1595*, 2002

McAdam, Ian, 'Carnal Identity in *The Jew of Malta*', *ELR* 26 (1996), 46–74

MacLure, Millar, ed., *Marlowe: The Critical Heritage 1588–1896*, 1979

Maguin, Jean-Marie, '*The Jew of Malta*: Marlowe's Ideological Stance and the Playworld's Ethos', *CE* 27 (1985), 17–26

Minshull, Catherine, 'Marlowe's "Sound Machevill"', *RenD* 13 (1982), 35–53

Palmer, Daryl W., 'Merchants and Miscegenation: *The Three Ladies of London*, *The Jew of Malta* and *The Merchant of Venice*', in Joyce MacDonald, ed., *Race, Ethnicity, and Power in the Renaissance*, 1997

Riggs, David, *The World of Christopher Marlowe*, 2004

Rothstein, Eric, 'Structure as Meaning in *The Jew of Malta*', *JEGP* 65 (1966), 260-73

Shapiro, James, *Rival Playwrights: Marlowe, Jonson, and Shakespeare*, 1991
————, *Shakespeare and the Jews*, 1996

Shepherd, Simon, *Marlowe and the Politics of Elizabethan Theatre*, 1986

Smith, James L., '*The Jew of Malta* in the Theatre', in Brian Morris, ed., *Christopher Marlowe*, 1968

Tambling, Jeremy, 'Abigail's Party: "The Difference of Things" in *The Jew of Malta*' in Dorothea Kehler and Susan Baker, eds., *In Another Country: Feminist Perspectives on Renaissance Drama*, 1991

Thomas, Vivien and William Tydeman, eds., *Christopher Marlowe: The Plays and their Sources*, 1994; rpt. 1999

Thurn, David H., 'Economic and Ideological Exchange in Marlowe's *Jew of Malta*', *TJ* 46 (1994), 157–70

Tromly, Frederic B., *Playing with Desire: Christopher Marlowe and the Art of Tantalization*, 1998

Weil, Judith, *Christopher Marlowe: Merlin's Prophet*, 1977

Wilson, Richard, ed., *Christopher Marlowe*, 1999

# ABBREVIATIONS

The first quarto edition of *The Jew of Malta* (1633) is referred to as Q. Other abbreviations are as follows:

EDITIONS

| | |
|---|---|
| Bawcutt | N. W. Bawcutt, ed., *The Jew of Malta* (Revels Plays), 1978 |
| Bennett | H. S. Bennett, ed., *The Jew of Malta and The Massacre at Paris*, 1931 |
| Bowers | Fredson Bowers, ed., *The Complete Works of Christopher Marlowe*, 1981 |
| Craik | T. W. Craik, ed., *The Jew of Malta* (New Mermaids), 3rd impression, 1979 |
| Steane | J. B. Steane, ed., *The Complete Plays of Christopher Marlowe*, 1969 |
| Van Fossen | Richard W. Van Fossen, ed., *The Jew of Malta* (Regents), 1964 |

PERIODICALS

| | |
|---|---|
| *CE* | *Cahiers Elisabéthains* |
| *ELH* | *English Literary History* |
| *ELR* | *English Literary Renaissance* |
| *JEGP* | *Journal of English and Germanic Philology* |
| *JWCI* | *Journal of the Warburg and Courtauld Institutes* |
| *MLQ* | *Modern Language Quarterly* |
| *RenD* | *Renaissance Drama* |
| *RES* | *Review of English Studies* |
| *RORD* | *Research Opportunities in Renaissance Drama* |
| *SQ* | *Shakespeare Quarterly* |
| *ShakS* | *Shakespeare Studies* |
| *TJ* | *Theatre Journal* |
| *TJHSE* | *Transactions of the Jewish Historical Society of England* |
| *TLS* | *The Times Literary Supplement* |

MISCELLANEOUS

| | |
|---|---|
| Gentillet | Innocent Gentillet, *A Discourse Upon the Meanes of Well Governing . . . A Kingdom* (trans. Simon Patericke), 1602 |
| Hunter | G. K. Hunter, 'The Theology of Marlowe's *The Jew of Malta*', *JWCI* 27 (1964), 211–40 |
| Tilley | M. P. Tilley, *A Dictionary of the Proverbs in England in the Sixteenth and Seventeenth Centuries*, 1950 |

Biblical quotations are from *The Geneva Bible: A Facsimile of the 1560 Edition*, 1969. Shakespeare is quoted from David Bevington, ed., *The Complete Works of Shakespeare* (4th edition), 1992. Quotations from Kyd's *The Spanish Tragedy* are from the New Mermaid edition of J. R. Mulryne, 1989; quotations from *Dr Faustus* are from the New Mermaid edition of Roma Gill, 1989; otherwise, Marlowe quotations are from the edition of J. B. Steane, 1969.

# The Famous
# TRAGEDY
## OF
# THE RICH IEVV
### OF *MALTA.*

# AS IT WAS PLAYD
## BEFORE THE KING AND
## QVEENE, IN HIS MAJESTIES
Theatre at *White-Hall,* by her Majesties
Servants at the *Cock-pit.*

*Written by* CHRISTOPHER MARLO.

## LONDON;
Printed by *I. B.* for *Nicholas Vavasour,* and are to be sold
at his Shop in the Inner-Temple, neere the
Church. 1633.

# THE EPISTLE DEDICATORY

*To my worthy friend, Mr.* THOMAS HAMMON,
*of Gray's Inn, &c.*

This play, composed by so worthy an author as Mr. Marlo; and the
part of the Jew presented by so unimitable an actor as Mr. Allin,
being in this later age commended to the stage: as I ushered it unto
the Court, and presented it to the Cock-pit, with these Prologues
and Epilogues here inserted, so now being newly brought to the          5
press, I was loath it should be published without the ornament of
an Epistle; making choice of you unto whom to devote it; than
whom (of all those gentlemen and acquaintance, within the
compass of my long knowledge) there is none more able to tax
ignorance, or attribute right to merit. Sir, you have been pleased to    10
grace some of mine own works with your courteous patronage;
I hope this will not be the worse accepted, because commended by
me; over whom, none can claim more power or privilege than
yourself. I had no better a New-year's gift to present you with; receive
it therefore as a continuance of that inviolable obligement, by which,   15
he rests still engaged; who as he ever hath, shall always remain,

*Tuissimus:*

THO. HEYWOOD.

0.2     THOMAS HAMMON Heywood also dedicated two of his own plays to Hammon (Part II
         of *The Fair Maid of the West* (1631) and Part I of *The Iron Age* (1632)).
0.3     *Gray's Inn* one of the Inns of Court; a centre of legal training
  2     *Allin* Edward Alleyn (1566–1626), famous actor of the late sixteenth century; he first
         acted the roles of Tamburlaine, Faustus and Barabas.
  3     *ushered* introduced
  4     *Court* The title-page asserts that the play was performed 'before the King and Queen,
         in his Majesties Theatre at *White-Hall*'.
         *Cock-pit* located in Drury Lane, one of the two principal Caroline theatres (also
         known as The Phoenix)
  9     *tax* censure
 10     *right* just assessment
 15     *obligement* obligation
 17     *Tuissimus* (Latin) wholly yours

3

# THE PROLOGUE
## TO THE STAGE, AT THE COCK-PIT

We know not how our play may pass this stage,
But by the best of *poets in that age          * Marlo
The Malta Jew had being, and was made;
And he, then by the best of †actors played:          †Allin
In *Hero and Leander*, one did gain               5
A lasting memory: in *Tamburlaine*,
This *Jew*, with others many: th' other wan
The attribute of peerless, being a man
Whom we may rank with (doing no one wrong)
Proteus for shapes, and Roscius for a tongue,      10
So could he speak, so vary; nor is't hate
To merit in ‡him who doth personate         ‡Perkins
Our Jew this day, nor is it his ambition
To exceed, or equal, being of condition
More modest; this is all that he intends,         15
(And that too, at the urgence of some friends)
To prove his best, and if none here gainsay it,
The part he hath studied, and intends to play it.

4    *Allin* Edward Alleyn. See note to Epistle Dedicatory.
5    *Hero and Leander* Marlowe's erotic narrative poem, based on Musaeus and published in 1598
6    *Tamburlaine* Alleyn also played the title role in Marlowe's *Tamburlaine*.
7    *wan* won
10   *Proteus* a sea god of Greek myth with the power of changing shape
      *Roscius* Quintus Roscius Gallus (d. 62 B.C.), the most famous Roman comic actor; later associated with great acting generally
11–12 *hate / To merit* i.e. an expression of jealousy to praise
12   *Perkins* Richard Perkins (d. 1650), a famous actor of the Jacobean and Caroline stage, acting c. 1602–37
14   *condition* temperament
16   *urgence* solicitation
17   *prove* try
      *gainsay* oppose

# EPILOGUE

In graving, with Pygmalion to contend;
Or painting, with Apelles; doubtless the end
Must be disgrace: our actor did not so,
He only aimed to go, but not out-go.
Nor think that this day any prize was played,                    5
Here were no bets at all, no wagers laid;
All the ambition that his mind doth swell,
Is but to hear from you, (by me) 'twas well.

1   *graving* sculpture
    *Pygmalion* the mythic king of Cyprus who fell in love with a beautiful statue he
    made (see Ovid, *Metamorphoses* X); the type of the great artist
2   *Apelles* a Greek painter (4th century B.C.) of legendary skill
4   *out-go* surpass
5   *prize was played* contest was engaged in (from fencing)
6   *no wagers laid* Apparently bets were sometimes made on the relative merits of actors.

# THE PROLOGUE
## SPOKEN AT COURT

Gracious and great, that we so boldly dare,
('Mongst other plays that now in fashion are)
To present this; writ many years agone,
And in that age, thought second unto none;
We humbly crave your pardon: we pursue                    5
The story of a rich and famous Jew
Who lived in Malta: you shall find him still,
In all his projects, a sound Machevill;
And that's his character: he that hath past
So many censures, is now come at last                     10
To have your princely ears, grace you him; then
You crown the action, and renown the pen.


# EPILOGUE

It is our fear (dread Sovereign) we have been
Too tedious; neither can't be less than sin
To wrong your princely patience: if we have,
(Thus low dejected) we your pardon crave:
And if aught here offend your ear or sight,               5
We only act, and speak, what others write.

*Prologue*
7    *still* always
8    *sound* complete, thorough
     *Machevill* See note on p. 9.
10   *censures* criticisms.

*Epilogue*
1    *dread* revered
2    *can't* can it
4    *Thus low dejected* i.e. bowing

# DRAMATIS PERSONAE

MACHEVILL, *the Prologue*
BARABAS, *the Jew of Malta*
FERNEZE, *the Governor of Malta*
ITHAMORE, *a Turkish slave to Barabas*
SELIM-CALYMATH, *the Turkish leader, son of the Turkish Emperor*
CALLAPINE, *a Bashaw*
ABIGAIL, *the daughter of Barabas*
DON LODOWICK, *the Governor's son*
DON MATHIAS, *his friend and lover of Abigail*
KATHERINE, *the mother of Don Mathias*
MARTIN DEL BOSCO, *Vice-Admiral of Spain*
FRIAR JACOMO
FRIAR BERNARDINE
BELLAMIRA, *a courtesan*
PILIA-BORZA, *a thief in league with her*
ABBESS
NUN
*Two* MERCHANTS; *three* JEWS; KNIGHTS; BASHAWS; OFFICERS;
SLAVES; CITIZENS; *Turkish* SOLDIERS; MESSENGER; CARPENTERS

No list of *Dramatis Personae* is given by Q.

7

# THE JEW OF MALTA

## PROLOGUE

*[Enter]* MACHEVILL

MACHEVILL

Albeit the world think Machevill is dead,

Yet was his soul but flown beyond the Alps, *[handwritten: soul is barbaras'!]*

And now the Guise is dead, is come from France

To view this land, and frolic with his friends.

To some perhaps my name is odious, 5

But such as love me, guard me from their tongues,

And let them know that I am Machevill,

And weigh not men, and therefore not men's words:

Admired I am of those that hate me most.

Though some speak openly against my books, 10

Yet will they read me, and thereby attain

To Peter's chair: and when they cast me off,

Are poisoned by my climbing followers.

I count religion but a childish toy, *[handwritten: WOWZA!]*

And hold there is no sin but ignorance. 15

---

0.2   *MACHEVILL* ed. (Q *Macheuil*); rhyming with 'still' in Heywood's Court Prologue; here an embodiment of the spirit of Niccolò Machiavelli (1469–1527), understood as the essence of villainous self-interested calculation. The opinions of this stage figure diverge significantly from those to be found in Machiavelli's writings, and may be indebted to the anti-Machiavellian discourse of writers like Innocent Gentillet (see Minshull and Bawcutt).

3   *the Guise* Henri de Lorraine, third Duke of Guise (1550–88), Roman Catholic opponent of the Huguenots and, in 1572, director of the St Bartholomew's Day massacre (see Marlowe's *Massace at Paris*).

4   *this land* England (mocking the hope expressed in contemporary polemic (e.g. Gentillet) that political calculation would not contaminate England from the Continent)

5–6   Meaning unclear: either the devotees of Machiavellianism protect him from his critics or, more likely, the disciples follow Machiavelli's precepts while avoiding mention of his name.

8   *weigh* esteem

9   Even those who denounce Machiavelli admire him in secret.

12   *Peter's chair* the papacy

    *cast me off* i.e. abandon my precepts

14   *toy* trifle. Machiavelli actually took religion seriously as a factor of political life (see *Discourses* I.11–15), but his opponents often described his doctrine as atheism.

Birds of the air will tell of murders past?
I am ashamed to hear such fooleries:
Many will talk of title to a crown.
What right had Caesar to the empire?
Might first made kings, and laws were then most sure          20
When like the Draco's they were writ in blood.
Hence comes it, that a strong built citadel
Commands much more than letters can import:
Which maxima had Phalaris observed,
H'had never bellowed in a brazen bull                        25
Of great ones' envy; o'th' poor petty wites,
Let me be envied and not pitied!
But whither am I bound, I come not, I,
To read a lecture here in Britaine,
But to present the tragedy of a Jew,                         30
Who smiles to see how full his bags are crammed,
Which money was not got without my means.
I crave but this, grace him as he deserves,
And let him not be entertained the worse
Because he favours me.                    [*Exit*]          35

16    *past?* ed. (Q past;) Such anecdotes, in which birds reveal an otherwise hidden crime,
      are taken by Machevill to exemplify the force of superstition rather than to evidence
      Providential order.
19    Here Machevill follows Machiavelli, who argues that Caesar was actually little different
      from the villainous Catiline, but won praise through wealth and power (*Discourses* I.10).
21    *Draco's* ed. (Q *Drancus*) referring to an Athenian legislator of proverbial severity
22    Citadels are traditionally used by tyrants to dominate their subjects (Bawcutt); the
      value of citadels is ambiguous in Machiavelli: in *The Prince* (XX) they are accorded
      limited value against internal enemies, but in *Discourses* (II.24) their usefulness is
      criticized.
23–5  According to legend the Sicilian tyrant Phalaris was killed in the brazen bull he had
      employed to roast his enemies. The opposition here implied is that between an
      interest in letters as a weakness and the use of force as a ruler's only true strength.
24    *maxima* ed. (Q maxime) maxim
26    *ones'* ed. (Q ones)
      *wites* either 'wights' (people) or 'wits'
27    *envied . . . not pitied* proverbial (Tilley, E 177)
29    *Britaine* Either 'Britain' or 'Britainy' – apparently the forms were equivalent in Eliza-
      bethan usage (compare *Edward II* II.ii.42).
31    *crammed,* ed. (Q cramb'd)
32    The suggestion that Machiavellian tactics have economic implications is odd, but, as
      Bawcutt points out, in keeping with Gentillet's polemical version of Machiavellianism.
33    *grace* honour
35    *favours* either 'resembles' or 'sides with'

# [ACT I, SCENE i]

*Enter* BARABAS *in his counting-house,*
*with heaps of gold before him*

BARABAS

So that of thus much that return was made:
And of the third part of the Persian ships,
There was the venture summed and satisfied.
As for those Samnites, and the men of Uz,
That bought my Spanish oils, and wines of Greece,                    5
Here have I pursed their paltry silverlings.
Fie; what a trouble 'tis to count this trash.
Well fare the Arabians, who so richly pay
The things they traffic for with wedge of gold,
Whereof a man may easily in a day                                    10
Tell that which may maintain him all his life.
The needy groom that never fingered groat,
Would make a miracle of thus much coin:
But he whose steel-barred coffers are crammed full,
And all his lifetime hath been tired,                                15
Wearying his fingers' ends with telling it,
Would in his age be loath to labour so,
And for a pound to sweat himself to death:
Give me the merchants of the Indian mines,

---

1    BARABAS ed. (Q *Iew* throughout scene except in stage directions). The name Barabas
     is that of the criminal released in place of Jesus (Mark 15.7). This speech is remark-
     able for beginning a play in mid-sentence and for the resemblance of its catalogue
     of jewels to that found in the opening speech of the Jew Jonathas in the fifteenth-
     century Croxton *Play of the Sacrament*.
3    *summed and satisfied* reckoned up and paid off
4    *Samnites* ed. (Q *Samintes*) Central Italian people who fought Rome several times
     from 354 B.C. The reference to them combined with that to the biblical Uz (Job 1.1)
     and, subsequently, to Kirriah Jairim (after a c ty named in Joshua 15.9; Judges 18.12)
     suggests the extent of Barabas's trade, but also his polyglot associations of biblical
     and classical references and discourses.
6    *silverlings* (Q *silverbings*) silver coin equivalent to Jewish shekel
8    *Well fare* optative phrase: 'Good fortune to them' (compare V.i.61)
     *pay* ed. (Q pay,)
9    *traffic* trade
11   *Tell* Count
12   *groom* slave, servant
     *groat* coin of small value (compare IV.ii.107)

That trade in metal of the purest mould;                     20
The wealthy Moor, that in the Eastern rocks
Without control can pick his riches up,
And in his house heap pearl like pebble-stones;
Receive them free, and sell them by the weight,
Bags of fiery opals, sapphires, amethysts,                   25
Jacinths, hard topaz, grass-green emeralds,
Beauteous rubies, sparkling diamonds,
And seldseen costly stones of so great price,
As one of them indifferently rated,
And of a caract of this quantity,                            30
May serve in peril of calamity
To ransom great kings from captivity.
This is the ware wherein consists my wealth:
And thus methinks should men of judgement frame
Their means of traffic from the vulgar trade,               35    *-excess*
And as their wealth increaseth, so inclose                        *-vulgar*
Infinite riches in a little room.
But now how stands the wind?
Into what corner peers my halcyon's bill?
Ha, to the east? Yes: see how stands the vanes?             40
East and by south: why then I hope my ships
I sent for Egypt and the bordering isles
Are gotten up by Nilus' winding banks:
Mine argosy from Alexandria,
Loaden with spice and silks, now under sail,                45

20    *mould* constitution, character
22    *Without control* Without restraint
28    *seldseen* ed. (Q seildsene) seldom seen, rare
29    *rated* valued
30    *caract* ed. (Q Carrect) carat, measure of gem weight, or possibly sign of character
      (compare *Measure for Measure* V.i.59). This semantic ambiguity of quantity and
      quality is potentially significant in a work with such economic interests and such
      insistent punning.
34    *frame* define, distinguish
37    *Infinite riches in a little room* Hunter defines this as a parody of traditional Christian
      imagery concerning the Virgin Birth; however, the phrase is also proverbial for great
      worth in a humble package (Tilley, W 921).
39    *halcyon* kingfisher, when dead and hung up, supposed to act as a weather vane
40    *stands* As frequently in Marlowe, singulars and plurals are interchangeable; compare
      lines 46 and 109.
41    *East and by south* i.e. south-east
44    *argosy* large merchant ship

Are smoothly gliding down by Candy shore
To Malta, through our Mediterranean sea.
But who comes here? How now.

*Enter a* MERCHANT

MERCHANT
Barabas, thy ships are safe,
Riding in Malta road: and all the merchants                    50
With other merchandise are safe arrived,
And have sent me to know whether yourself
Will come and custom them.
BARABAS
The ships are safe thou say'st, and richly fraught?
MERCHANT
They are.
BARABAS          Why then go bid them come ashore,          55
And bring with them their bills of entry:
I hope our credit in the custom-house
Will serve as well as I were present there.
Go send 'em three score camels, thirty mules,
And twenty waggons to bring up the ware.                       60
But art thou master in a ship of mine,
And is thy credit not enough for that?
MERCHANT
The very custom barely comes to more
Than many merchants of the town are worth,
And therefore far exceeds my credit, sir.                      65
BARABAS
Go tell 'em the Jew of Malta sent thee, man:
Tush, who amongst 'em knows not Barabas?
MERCHANT
I go.

---

46  *Candy* Crete
48  *But who comes here?* a formula for dramatic entry already archaic in Marlowe's day,
    but in keeping with some of the other stylistic qualities of the play
50  *road* ed. (Q Rhode) harbour
53  *custom* see them through customs procedures
54  *fraught* loaded with merchandise
63  *very custom barely* the duties alone

BARABAS

So then, there's somewhat come.

Sirrah, which of my ships art thou master of?                              70

MERCHANT

Of the Speranza, sir.

BARABAS                           And saw'st thou not

Mine argosy at Alexandria?

Thou couldst not come from Egypt, or by Caire

But at the entry there into the sea,

Where Nilus pays his tribute to the main.                                  75

Thou needs must sail by Alexandria.

MERCHANT

I neither saw them, nor inquired of them.

But this we heard some of our seamen say,

They wondered how you durst with so much wealth

Trust such a crazèd vessel, and so far.                                    80

BARABAS

Tush; they are wise, I know her and her strength:

But go, go thou thy ways, discharge thy ship,

And bid my factor bring his loading in.

                                              [*Exit* MERCHANT]

And yet I wonder at this argosy.

*Enter a* SECOND MERCHANT

2 MERCHANT

Thine argosy from Alexandria,                                             85

Know Barabas doth ride in Malta road,

Laden with riches, and exceeding store

Of Persian silks, of gold, and orient pearl.

BARABAS

How chance you came not with those other ships

    70   *Sirrah* a contemptuous form of address

           *master of* ed. (Q Master off)

 71–2   ed. (Q And . . . Alexandria? / Thou)

    73   *Caire* Cairo

    80   *crazèd* unseaworthy

    81   *they are wise* sarcastic

    82   *But* ed. (Q By)

           *go thou thy ways* i.e. be off!

    83   *factor* agent

           *loading* cargo

    88   *orient* from the East, brilliant

That sailed by Egypt?

2 MERCHANT                     Sir we saw 'em not.            90

BARABAS

Belike they coasted round by Candy shore
About their oils, or other businesses.
But 'twas ill done of you to come so far
Without the aid or conduct of their ships.

2 MERCHANT

Sir, we were wafted by a Spanish fleet            95
That never left us till within a league,
That had the galleys of the Turk in chase.

BARABAS

Oh they were going up to Sicily: well, go
And bid the merchants and my men dispatch
And come ashore, and see the fraught discharged.     100

2 MERCHANT

I go.                                    *Exit*

BARABAS

Thus trowls our fortune in by land and sea,
And thus are we on every side enriched:
These are the blessings promised to the Jews,
And herein was old Abram's happiness:           105
What more may heaven do for earthly man
Than thus to pour out plenty in their laps,
Ripping the bowels of the earth for them,
Making the sea their servant, and the winds
To drive their substance with successful blasts?      110

---

91     *Belike* Perhaps
94     *conduct* escort
95     *wafted* escorted
96     *within a league* i.e. within approximately 3 miles of our destination
97     *in chase* in pursuit
102    *trowls* rolls in
104–5   This refers to God's covenant with Abraham. This blessing from Genesis 15 is claimed by Christian theologians who, like Luther, assert that Jews misinterpret the divine blessing by 'applying it only to a carnal blessing, and do great injury to Scripture' (*Commentary on Galatians* (English ed. 1575)); see Hunter on Galatians 3.13–16; compare II.iii.47. The passage also echoes Ovid's description of the Age of Iron, as Bawcutt points out.
109    *servant* ed. (Q servants) Singulars and plurals are a source of difficulty from line 106 on.
109–10   *the winds . . . blasts* i.e. the winds propel the ships that carry their goods

Who hateth me but for my happiness?
Or who is honoured now but for his wealth?
Rather had I a Jew be hated thus,
Than pitied in a Christian poverty:
For I can see no fruits in all their faith,                              115
But malice, falsehood, and excessive pride,
Which methinks fits not their profession.
Happily some hapless man hath conscience,
And for his conscience lives in beggary.
They say we are a scattered nation:                                      120
I cannot tell, but we have scambled up
More wealth by far than those that brag of faith.
There's Kirriah Jairim, the great Jew of Greece,
Obed in Bairseth, Nones in Portugal,
Myself in Malta, some in Italy,                                          125
Many in France, and wealthy every one:
Ay, wealthier far than any Christian.
I must confess we come not to be kings:
That's not our fault: alas, our number's few,
And crowns come either by succession,                                    130
Or urged by force; and nothing violent,
Oft have I heard tell, can be permanent.
Give us a peaceful rule, make Christians kings,
That thirst so much for principality.
I have no charge, nor many children,                                     135
But one sole daughter, whom I hold as dear

111   *happiness* prosperity
115   *fruits . . . faith* common New Testament image (see John 15.1–6; compare Kocher,
      pp. 124–5)
117   *profession* religious faith
118   *Happily some hapless* haply, perhaps some unfortunate
120   *scattered nation* referring to belief that Jewish dispersal reflected God's anger
121   *scambled up* raked together, perhaps rapaciously
123   *Kirriah Jairim* personal name after a biblical city (see 4n.)
124   *Obed* the child of Ruth and Boaz, and ancestor of Jesus, 'notwithstanding', as the
      Geneva Bible gloss says, that Ruth was 'a Moabite of base condicion, and a stranger
      from the people of God' (Ruth 1, 'argument')
      *Bairseth* not identified
      *Nones* perhaps derived from the name of Dr Hector Nunez, a prominent member
      of the marrano community in London
128   *come not to be* do not become
131–2 *nothing . . . permanent* proverbial (see Gentillet, pp. 13, 200, 316)
134   *principality* rule
135   *charge* responsibility

16

As Agamemnon did his Iphigen:    LOL
And all I have is hers. But who comes here?

*Enter* THREE JEWS

1 JEW

Tush, tell not me 'twas done of policy.

2 JEW

Come therefore let us go to Barabas;                    140
For he can counsel best in these affairs;
And here he comes.

BARABAS                    Why how now countrymen?
Why flock you thus to me in multitudes?
What accident's betided to the Jews?

1 JEW

A fleet of warlike galleys, Barabas,                    145
Are come from Turkey, and lie in our road:
And they this day sit in the council-house
To entertain them and their embassy.

BARABAS

Why let 'em come, so they come not to war;
Or let 'em war, so we be conquerors.                    150
(Nay, let 'em combat, conquer, and kill all,
So they spare me, my daughter, and my wealth.)

1 JEW

Were it for confirmation of a league,
They would not come in warlike manner thus.

2 JEW

I fear their coming will afflict us all.                    155

BARABAS

Fond men, what dream you of their multitudes?

137    Ironic, since Agamemnon was forced to sacrifice his daughter Iphigenia to obtain a
        favourable wind for the Greek military expedition against Troy.
139    *policy* cunning politics; often used pejoratively during the Renaissance to refer to
        Machiavellian deviousness
144    *betided to* happening to
147    *they* the rulers of Malta
151    ed. (Q has a marginal '*aside*') This is the first of Barabas's many lines spoken only in
        part to his on-stage interlocutors. The precise limits of the aside portions of his lines
        are often ambiguous. However, it often appears that they are the final words or
        phrases which serve to modify or contradict what precedes them. Asides are marked
        in the present edition by parentheses.
156    *Fond* Foolish

What need they treat of peace that are in league?
The Turks and those of Malta are in league.
Tut, tut, there is some other matter in't.

**1 JEW**

Why, Barabas, they come for peace or war.                    160

**BARABAS**

Happily for neither, but to pass along
Towards Venice by the Adriatic Sea;
With whom they have attempted many times,
But never could effect their stratagem.

**3 JEW**

And very wisely said, it may be so.                          165

**2 JEW**

But there's a meeting in the senate-house,
And all the Jews in Malta must be there.

**BARABAS**

Umh; all the Jews in Malta must be there?
Ay, like enough, why then let every man
Provide him, and be there for fashion-sake.                  170
If any thing shall there concern our state
Assure yourselves I'll look (unto myself).

**1 JEW**

I know you will; well brethren let us go.

**2 JEW**

Let's take our leaves; farewell good Barabas.

**BARABAS**

Do so; farewell Zaareth, farewell Temainte.                  175

[*Exeunt* JEWS]

And Barabas now search this secret out.
Summon thy senses, call thy wits together:
These silly men mistake the matter clean

---

157    *in league* in agreement
163    *With whom* against whom
168    *Umh* a noise indicating reflectiveness
170    *Provide him . . . for fashion-sake* Get ready . . . according to form
171    *our state* the material conditions of Jews or their collective standing as a defined
       class or group
172    ed. (Q has a marginal *'aside'*)
175    *Temainte* perhaps a reminiscence of Eliphaz the Temanite, one of Job's comforters
       (Job 2)
178    *silly* simple, innocent
       *clean* completely

Long to the Turk did Malta contribute;
Which tribute all in policy, I fear,                                          180
The Turks have let increase to such a sum,
As all the wealth of Malta cannot pay;
And now by that advantage thinks, belike,
To seize upon the town: ay, that he seeks.
Howe'er the world go, I'll make sure for one,                    185
And seek in time to intercept the worst,
Warily guarding that which I ha' got.
*Ego mihimet sum semper proximus.*
Why let 'em enter, let 'em take the town.                    [*Exit*]

---

185   *make . . . one* look out for myself
186   *intercept* prevent
188   *Ego . . . proximus* adapted from Terence's *Andria*, 'Proximus sum egomet mihi,'
        (IV.i.12), 'I am always nearest to myself'

# [ACT I, SCENE ii]

*Enter* [FERNEZE,] GOVERNOR *of Malta,* KNIGHTS
[*and* OFFICERS,] *met by* BASHAWS *of the Turk;* CALYMATH

FERNEZE

  Now bashaws, what demand you at our hands?

BASHAW

  Know knights of Malta, that we came from Rhodes,
  From Cyprus, Candy, and those other isles
  That lie betwixt the Mediterranean seas.

FERNEZE

  What's Cyprus, Candy, and those other isles                    5
  To us, or Malta? What at our hands demand ye?

CALYMATH

  The ten years' tribute that remains unpaid.

FERNEZE

  Alas, my lord, the sum is over-great,
  I hope your highness will consider us.

CALYMATH

  I wish, grave Governor, 'twere in my power                     10
  To favour you, but 'tis my father's cause,
  Wherein I may not, nay I dare not dally.

FERNEZE

  Then give us leave, great Selim-Calymath.

CALYMATH

  Stand all aside, and let the knights determine,

0.1   GOVERNOR Throughout this scene (e.g. lines 10, 17, 32) Q uses the plural, while the
      speech heading for the speaker who leads the Maltese Knights is 'Governor'. As in the
      case of 'Jew' in I.i, a general designation is subsequently replaced w th a proper name;
      by II.ii the leader of Malta is 'Ferneze'.
      KNIGHTS members of the Order of St John of Jerusalem

0.2   BASHAWS ed. (Q BASSOES) pashas, Turkish military functionaries

4     seas The Adriatic, Aegean, etc. Many editors insert a dash here for Q's full stop to
      reinforce the idea that Ferneze interrupts the Bashaw's oratory.

9     consider grant consideration to

10    grave worthy of respect
      Governor, ed. (Q Governors)

13    give us leave allow us private conference
      Selim-Calymath Selim was the name of the son of Suleiman the Magnificent, Turkish
      ruler during the siege of Malta in 1565.

And send to keep our galleys under sail,           15
For happily we shall not tarry here:
Now Governor how are you resolved?

FERNEZE

Thus: since your hard conditions are such
That you will needs have ten years' tribute past,
We may have time to make collection           20
Amongst the inhabitants of Malta for't.

BASHAW

That's more than is in our commission.

CALYMATH

What Callapine a little courtesy.
Let's know their time, perhaps it is not long;
And 'tis more kingly to obtain by peace           25
Than to enforce conditions by constraint.
What respite ask you Governor?

FERNEZE                        But a month.

CALYMATH

We grant a month, but see you keep your promise.
Now launch our galleys back again to sea,
Where we'll attend the respite you have ta'en,       30
And for the money send our messenger.
Farewell great Governor, and brave knights of Malta.

*Exeunt* [CALYMATH *and* BASHAWS]

FERNEZE

And all good fortune wait on Calymath.
Go one and call those Jews of Malta hither:
Were they not summoned to appear today?         35

OFFICER

They were, my lord, and here they come.

*Enter* BARABAS *and* THREE JEWS

1 KNIGHT

Have you determined what to say to them?

FERNEZE

Yes, give me leave, and Hebrews now come near.
From the Emperor of Turkey is arrived

---

14   *Stand all aside* Give them room
17   *how . . . resolved?* What have you decided?
22   *than . . . commission* than we are authorized to do
35   *today?* ed. (Q to day.)

Great Selim-Calymath, his highness' son,                                    40
To levy of us ten years' tribute past,
Now then here know that it concerneth us:

BARABAS

Then good my lord, to keep your quiet still,
Your Lordship shall do well to let them have it.

FERNEZE

Soft Barabas, there's more longs to't than so.                             45
To what this ten years' tribute will amount,
That we have cast, but cannot compass it
By reason of the wars, that robbed our store;
And therefore are we to request your aid.

BARABAS

Alas, my Lord, we are no soldiers:                                          50
And what's our aid against so great a prince?

1 KNIGHT

Tut, Jew, we know thou art no soldier;
Thou art a merchant, and a moneyed man,
And 'tis thy money, Barabas, we seek.

BARABAS

How, my lord, my money?

FERNEZE                                    Thine and the rest.              55
For to be short, amongst you't must be had.

1 JEW

Alas, my lord, the most of us are poor!

FERNEZE

Then let the rich increase your portions:

BARABAS

Are strangers with your tribute to be taxed?

2 KNIGHT

Have strangers leave with us to get their wealth?                          60

---

42   Q's punctuation is a colon, which Ethel Seaton argues ('Marlowe's Map', *Essays and Studies* 10 (1924)) may signal 'rhetorical upward intonation' (p. 31); thus it may be suggested that Barabas interrupts Ferneze before he has completed his statement (compare line 58).

43   *keep . . . still* preserve your peace

45   *longs* belongs, pertains

46   *amount,* ed. (Q amount)

47   *cast . . . compass* calculated but cannot satisfy

48   *store* treasury

57   *1 JEW* ed. (Q *Iew*)

58   *increase your portions* contribute for you

59   *strangers* foreigners

Then let them with us contribute.

BARABAS

How, equally?

FERNEZE                No, Jew, like infidels.

For through our sufferance of your hateful lives,

Who stand accursèd in the sight of heaven,

These taxes and afflictions are befallen,                                65

And therefore thus we are determinèd;

Read there the articles of our decrees.

OFFICER [*Reading*]

First, the tribute money of the Turks shall all be levied amongst the Jews, and each of them to pay one half of his estate.                                                              70

BARABAS

How, half his estate? I hope you mean not mine.

FERNEZE

Read on.

OFFICER [*Reading*]

Secondly, he that denies to pay, shall straight become a Christian.

BARABAS

How, a Christian? Hum, what's here to do?                 75

OFFICER [*Reading*]

Lastly, he that denies this, shall absolutely lose all he has.

ALL 3 JEWS

Oh my lord we will give half.

BARABAS

Oh earth-metalled villains, and no Hebrews born!

And will you basely thus submit yourselves                80

To leave your goods to their arbitrament?

FERNEZE

Why Barabas wilt thou be christened?

---

 64    *accursèd* i.e. for a role in the Crucifixion of Christ (cf. Matthew 27.25, and line 108)
 66    *determinèd* resolved
 68    OFFICER [*Reading*] ed. (Q *Reader* as at lines 73, 76)
68–70   ed. (Q First . . . be / Leuyed . . . one / Halfe . . . estate.)
 71    Many editors make all or part of this and line 75 asides.
73–4   ed. (Q Secondly . . . become / A Christian.)
76–7   ed. (Q *one line*)
 79    *earth-metalled* base, dull in temperament
 81    *arbitrament* disposal

BARABAS

No, Governor, I will be no convertite.

FERNEZE

Then pay thy half.

BARABAS

Why know you what you did by this device?                    85
Half of my substance is a city's wealth.
Governor, it was not got so easily;
Nor will I part so slightly therewithal.

FERNEZE

Sir, half is the penalty of our decree,
Either pay that, or we will seize on all.                    90

BARABAS

*Corpo di Dio*; stay, you shall have half,
Let me be used but as my brethren are.

FERNEZE

No, Jew, thou hast denied the articles,
And now it cannot be recalled.

                                  [*Exeunt* OFFICERS]

BARABAS

Will you then steal my goods?                                95
Is theft the ground of your religion?

FERNEZE

No, Jew, we take particularly thine
To save the ruin of a multitude:
And better one want for a common good,
Than many perish for a private man:                          100
Yet Barabas we will not banish thee,
But here in Malta, where thou got'st thy wealth,
Live still; and if thou canst, get more.

BARABAS

Christians, what or how can I multiply?
Of nought is nothing made.                                   105

85    Craik suggests an echo of Christ's 'They knowe not what they do' (Luke 23.34).
88    *slightly* easily, without resistance
91    *Corpo di Dio* (Italian) Body of God!
94    Many editors have the officers exit here to seize Barabas's wealth; they apparently re-
      enter at line 131.
96    *ground* basis
99–100 Hunter suggests an echo of John 11.50.
100   *private* individual
105   proverbial; but also potentially a point of contention between Aristotelian and
      biblical thinking concerning Creation

1 KNIGHT

    From nought at first thou cam'st to little wealth,
    From little unto more, from more to most:
    If your first curse fall heavy on thy head,
    And make thee poor and scorned of all the world,
    'Tis not our fault, but thy inherent sin.           110

BARABAS

    What? Bring you scripture to confirm your wrongs?
    Preach me not out of my possessions.
    Some Jews are wicked, as all Christians are:
    But say the tribe that I descended of
    Were all in general cast away for sin,           115
    Shall I be tried by their transgression?
    The man that dealeth righteously shall live:
    And which of you can charge me otherwise?

FERNEZE

    Out wretched Barabas,
    Sham'st thou not thus to justify thyself,         120
    As if we knew not thy profession?
    If thou rely upon thy righteousness,
    Be patient and thy riches will increase.
    Excess of wealth is cause of covetousness:
    And covetousness, oh 'tis a monstrous sin.      125

BARABAS

    Ay, but theft is worse: tush, take not from me then,
    For that is theft; and if you rob me thus,
    I must be forced to steal and compass more.

1 KNIGHT

    Grave Governor, list not to his exclaims:
    Convert his mansion to a nunnery,           130

108    *your first curse* i.e. that of the Jews (compare line 64)
         *thy* The shift in pronouns suggests a move from the racially general ('your') to the individual.
113    *as all Christians are* possibly an aside
115    *cast away* rejected by God
117    Compare Proverbs 10.2 ('The treasures of wickednes profite nothing: but righteousnes deliuereth from death') and 12.28.
119–22  ed. (Q Out . . . thus / To . . . not / Thy . . . righteousnesse,)
119    *Out* an expression of reproach
121    *profession* religious creed (compare line 146), personal code or occupation – i.e. as merchant or as usurer
128    *compass* contrive to attain
129    *exclaims* exclamations

*Enter* OFFICERS

His house will harbour many holy nuns.

FERNEZE

It shall be so: now officers, have you done?

OFFICER

Ay, my lord, we have seized upon the goods
And wares of Barabas, which being valued
Amount to more than all the wealth in Malta.                     135
And of the other we have seizèd half.
Then we'll take order for the residue.

BARABAS

Well then my lord, say, are you satisfied?
You have my goods, my money, and my wealth,
My ships, my store, and all that I enjoyed;                      140
And having all, you can request no more;
Unless your unrelenting flinty hearts
Suppress all pity in your stony breasts,
And now shall move you to bereave my life.

FERNEZE

No, Barabas, to stain our hands with blood                       145
Is far from us and our profession.

BARABAS

Why, I esteem the injury far less,
To take the lives of miserable men,
Than be the causers of their misery.
You have my wealth, the labour of my life,                       150
The comfort of mine age, my children's hope,
And therefore ne'er distinguish of the wrong.

FERNEZE

Content thee, Barabas, thou hast nought but right.

BARABAS

Your extreme right does me exceeding wrong:

---

136    *the other* the other Jews
137    *the residue* the balance of the tribute or the rest of the affair
146    *profession* Christian principles (compare line 121)
147    *Why,* ed. (Q Why)
150    *wealth,* ed. (Q wealth)
152    *distinguish of the wrong* draw false distinctions between murder and theft
153    *nought but right* nothing but justice
154    proverbial (Tilley, R 122), but also, of course, a potential nexus for one version of classical tragedy

But take it to you i' the devil's name.　　'　　155

FERNEZE

Come, let us in, and gather of these goods
The money for this tribute of the Turk.

1 KNIGHT

'Tis necessary that be looked unto:
For if we break our day, we break the league,
And that will prove but simple policy.　　160

*Exeunt [all except* BARABAS *and* JEWS]

BARABAS

Ay, policy? that's their profession,
And not simplicity, as they suggest.　　　　*[Kneels]*
The plagues of Egypt, and the curse of heaven,
Earth's barrenness, and all men's hatred
Inflict upon them, thou great *Primus Motor.*　　165
And here upon my knees, striking the earth,
I ban their souls to everlasting pains
And extreme tortures of the fiery deep,
That thus have dealt with me in my distress.

*get back at them*

1 JEW

Oh yet be patient, gentle Barabas.　　　　170

BARABAS

Oh silly brethren, born to see this day!
Why stand you thus unmoved with my laments?
Why weep you not to think upon my wrongs?
Why pine not I, and die in this distress?

---

155　*i'the* ed. (Q i'th')
159　*break our day* miss our deadline
160　*simple policy* foolish strategy
161–2　*Ay, policy? . . . simplicity* Picking up the phrase 'simple policy', Barabas offers an analysis of the hypocrisy of the Maltese Christians, who profess Christian honesty – 'the simplicitie that is in Christ' (II Corinthians 11.3) – but practice cunning strategy.
162　*Kneels* Barabas is clearly on his knees by line 166 and probably refers to his posture at line 172. His kneeling is one of this scene's many echoes of the dramaturgy of *The Spanish Tragedy.* The point at which he rises is not clear, but Bawcutt's suggestion of line 215 makes sense.
163　*plagues of Egypt* described in Exodus 7–12
165　*Primus Motor* (Latin) First Mover, 'The chiefest God' of *I Tamburlaine* IV.ii.8–9 and Aristotle's *Metaphysics*
167　*ban* curse
171　*silly* foolish
172–4　As Craik points out, the patterned repetition of these lines resembles stylistic devices of *The Spanish Tragedy*; see also III.iii.42–9 and III.v.35–6.

1 JEW

    Why, Barabas, as hardly can we brook             175

    The cruel handling of ourselves in this:

    Thou seest they have taken half our goods.

BARABAS

    Why did you yield to their extortion?

    You were a multitude, and I but one,

    And of me only have they taken all.               180

1 JEW

    Yet brother Barabas remember Job.

BARABAS

    What tell you me of Job? I wot his wealth

    Was written thus: he had seven thousand sheep,

    Three thousand camels, and two hundred yoke

    Of labouring oxen, and five hundred           185

    She-asses: but for every one of those,

    Had they been valued at indifferent rate,

    I had at home, and in mine argosy

    And other ships that came from Egypt last,

    As much as would have bought his beasts and him,    190

    And yet have kept enough to live upon;

    So that not he, but I may curse the day,

    Thy fatal birthday, forlorn Barabas;

    And henceforth wish for an eternal night,

    That clouds of darkness may enclose my flesh,      195

    And hide these extreme sorrows from mine eyes:

    For only I have toiled to inherit here

    The months of vanity and loss of time,

    And painful nights have been appointed me.

---

175    *brook* endure

182    *wot* know

182–208    These lines frequently echo chapters 1, 3 and 7 of the Book of Job. Lines 192–6 are very closely related to Job 3.1–10: 'Afterward Iob opened his mouthe, and cursed his day. And Iob cryed out, and said, Let the daye perish, wherein I was borne, and the night when it was said, There is a manchilde conceiued. Let that day be darkenes, let not God regarde it from above, nether let the light shine vpon it, But let darkenes, & the shadowe of death staine it: let the cloude remaine vpon it, & let them make it fearefull as a bitter day . . . Because it shut not vp the dores of my mothers wombe: nor hid sorowe from mine eyes.' Similarly close relationships exist in lines 197–9 to Job 7.3 and in line 208 to Job 7.11.

187    *at indifferent rate* impartially evaluated

2 JEW

Good Barabas be patient.                                        200

BARABAS

Ay, I pray leave me in my patience.
You that were ne'er possessed of wealth, are pleased with want.
But give him liberty at least to mourn,
That in a field amidst his enemies,
Doth see his soldiers slain, himself disarmed,        205
And knows no means of his recovery:
Ay, let me sorrow for this sudden chance;
'Tis in the trouble of my spirit I speak;
Great injuries are not so soon forgot.

1 JEW

Come, let us leave him in his ireful mood,            210
Our words will but increase his ecstasy.

2 JEW

On then: but trust me 'tis a misery
To see a man in such affliction:
Farewell Barabas.

                                        *Exeunt* [JEWS]

BARABAS

Ay, fare you well.                                             215
See the simplicity of these base slaves,
Who for the villains have no wit themselves,
Think me to be a senseless lump of clay
That will with every water wash to dirt:
No, Barabas is born to better chance,                215
And framed of finer mould than common men,
That measure nought but by the present time.
A reaching thought will search his deepest wits,
And cast with cunning for the time to come:

201    *Ay, I* ed. (Q I, I)
210    *ireful* enraged
211    *ecstasy* passion
216–17   *simplicity . . . base slaves . . . villains* Barabas changes tone abruptly, condescending
          to the departed Jews as foolish, socially inferior and debased generally.
219    *with every water wash to dirt* fall into disarray at any sort of trouble
220    *chance* fortune
221    *mould* earth
223    *reaching thought* penetrating analyst
224    *cast with cunning* wisely anticipate

For evils are apt to happen every day.                    225
But whither wends my beauteous Abigail?

*Enter* ABIGAIL *the Jew's daughter*

Oh what has made my lovely daughter sad?
What? Woman, moan not for a little loss:
Thy father has enough in store for thee.

ABIGAIL

Not for myself, but agèd Barabas:                          230
Father, for thee lamenteth Abigail:
But I will learn to leave these fruitless tears,
And urged thereto with my afflictions,
With fierce exclaims run to the senate-house,
And in the senate reprehend them all,                      235
And rent their hearts with tearing of my hair,
Till they reduce the wrongs done to my father.

BARABAS

No, Abigail, things past recovery
Are hardly cured with exclamations.
Be silent, daughter, sufferance breeds ease,               240
And time may yield us an occasion
Which on the sudden cannot serve the turn.
Besides, my girl, think me not all so fond
As negligently to forgo so much
Without provision for thyself and me.                       245
Ten thousand portagues, besides great pearls,
Rich costly jewels, and stones infinite,
Fearing the worst of this before it fell,
I closely hid.

ABIGAIL          Where father?

BARABAS                          In my house my girl.

---

226    *Abigail* On the association of the biblical Abiga l (I Samuel 25) with conversion to
       Christianity, see Hunter, p. 225.
236    *rent* rend, tear
238–9  *things past . . . exclamations* proverbial (Tilley, C 921, 'past cure, past care')
240    *sufferance . . . ease* proverbial (Tilley, S 955)
       *sufferance breeds* 'patient endurance teaches'
241–2  *And time . . . turn* time may eventually present us with a better opportunity than
       now it offers
243    *fond* foolish
246    *portagues* Portuguese gold coins

ABIGAIL

    Then shall they ne'er be seen of Barabas:           250
    For they have seized upon thy house and wares.

BARABAS

    But they will give me leave once more, I trow,
    To go into my house.

ABIGAIL             That may they not:

    For there I left the Governor placing nuns,
    Displacing me; and of thy house they mean         255
    To make a nunnery, where none but their own sect
    Must enter in; men generally barred.

BARABAS

    My gold, my gold, and all my wealth is gone.
    You partial heavens, have I deserved this plague?
    What will you thus oppose me, luckless stars,       260
    To make me desperate in my poverty?
    And knowing me impatient in distress
    Think me so mad as I will hang myself,
    That I may vanish o'er the earth in air,
    And leave no memory that e'er I was?         265
    No, I will live; nor loathe I this my life:
    And since you leave me in the ocean thus
    To sink or swim, and put me to my shifts,
    I'll rouse my senses, and awake myself.
    Daughter, I have it: thou perceiv'st the plight     270
    Wherein these Christians have oppressèd me:
    Be ruled by me, for in extremity
    We ought to make bar of no policy.

ABIGAIL

    Father, whate'er it be to injure them
    That have so manifestly wrongèd us,          275
    What will not Abigail attempt?

BARABAS             Why so;

---

252   *trow* trust
256   *sect* sex, but perhaps resonant with the many references to sectarian division according to religion
259   *partial* biased
260   *luckless* malignant
268   *put me . . . shifts* force me to fend for myself. Both this and 'sink or swim' are proverbial (Tilley, S 485; S 337).
273   *make bar . . . policy* rule out no strategy

Then thus, thou told'st me they have turned my house
Into a nunnery, and some nuns are there.

ABIGAIL
I did.

BARABAS          Then Abigail, there must my girl
Entreat the abbess to be entertained.                              280

ABIGAIL
How, as a nun?

BARABAS          Ay, daughter, for religion
Hides many mischiefs from suspicion.

ABIGAIL
Ay, but father they will suspect me there.

BARABAS
Let 'em suspect, but be thou so precise
As they may think it done of holiness.                             285
Entreat 'em fair, and give them friendly speech,
And seem to them as if thy sins were great,
Till thou hast gotten to be entertained.

ABIGAIL
Thus father shall I much dissemble.

BARABAS                              Tush,
As good dissemble that thou never mean'st                          290
As first mean truth and then dissemble it;
A counterfeit profession is better
Than unseen hypocrisy.

ABIGAIL
Well father, say I be entertained,
What then shall follow?

276–7    ed. (Q Why . . . house / Into . . .)
280      *entertained* received, admitted as a nun
281–2    *religion . . . suspicion* Compare the relevant portions of Machiavelli's *Prince* con-
         cerning the political uses of religion (esp. chapter XVIII) with the statement of
         Machevill in the Prologue and with Gentillet's attacks on the 'atheism' of Machia-
         vellians; compare Minshull's analysis.
284      *precise* scrupulous; often pejoratively applied to Puritans
286      *Entreat 'em fair* present yourself ingratiatingly
289–90   ed. (Q Thus . . . dissemble. / Tush . . . mean'st)
290–1    *As good . . . dissemble it* It's no worse to deceive deliberately than to begin with true
         intentions and subsequently turn to hypocrisy
292–3    *A counterfeit profession . . . unseen hypocrisy* This passage seems to say that self-
         conscious religious hypocrisy is preferable to an unwitting ideological blindness;
         see Hodge.
294      *say* suppose

BARABAS                         This shall follow then;                    295
   There have I hid close underneath the plank
   That runs along the upper chamber floor,
   The gold and jewels which I kept for thee.
   But here they come; be cunning Abigail.

ABIGAIL
   Then father go with me.

BARABAS                         No, Abigail, in this                       300
   It is not necessary I be seen.
   For I will seem offended with thee for't.
   Be close, my girl, for this must fetch my gold.

*Enter three* FRIARS [JACOMO *and* BERNARDINE
*among them] and two* NUNS [*one the* ABBESS]

JACOMO
   Sisters, we now are almost at the new-made nunnery.

1 NUN
   The better; for we love not to be seen:                            305
   'Tis thirty winters long since some of us
   Did stray so far amongst the multitude.

JACOMO
   But, madam, this house
   And waters of this new-made nunnery
   Will much delight you.                                              310

1 NUN
   It may be so: but who comes here?

ABIGAIL
   Grave Abbess, and you happy virgins' guide,
   Pity the state of a distressèd maid.

ABBESS
   What art thou daughter?

ABIGAIL
   The hopeless daughter of a hapless Jew,                            315
   The Jew of Malta, wretched Barabas;

296   *close* secretly
301   It is necessary I should not be seen
304   JACOMO ed. (Q 1 *Fry.*)
312   *you happy virgins' guide* This portion of the line may be addressed to the friar.
315   Compare Hieronimo's line from *The Spanish Tragedy:* 'The hopeless father of a
      hapless son' (IV.iv.84).
      *hapless* unfortunate

Sometimes the owner of a goodly house,
Which they have now turned to a nunnery.

ABBESS

Well, daughter, say, what is thy suit with us?

ABIGAIL

Fearing the afflictions which my father feels                320
Proceed from sin, or want of faith in us,
I'd pass away my life in penitence,
And be a novice in your nunnery,
To make atonement for my labouring soul.

JACOMO

No doubt, brother, but this proceedeth of the spirit.        325

BERNARDINE

Ay, and of a moving spirit too, brother; but come,
Let us entreat she may be entertained.

ABBESS

Well, daughter, we admit you for a nun.

ABIGAIL

First let me as a novice learn to frame
My solitary life to your strait laws,                        330
And let me lodge where I was wont to lie;
I do not doubt by your divine precepts
And mine own industry, but to profit much.

BARABAS

(As much I hope as all I hid is worth.)

ABBESS

Come daughter, follow us.                                    335

BARABAS

Why how now Abigail, what mak'st thou
Amongst these hateful Christians?

JACOMO

Hinder her not, thou man of little faith,

317   *Sometimes* Sometime, formerly
320   *feels* ed. (*Q feels,*)
324   *labouring* struggling, troubled
325   *proceedeth of the spirit* comes of the Holy Spirit
326   *BERNARDINE* ed. (Q 2 *Fry.*)
      *moving* This and subsequent lines (see III.vi) permit interpretation in a sexual sense.
330   *strait* strict, confining
331   *wont* accustomed
334   ed. (Q has a marginal '*aside*')
336   *what mak'st thou* what are you doing?
338   *thou man of little faith* biblical phrasing (e.g. Matthew 6.30, 8.26)

For she has mortified herself.

BARABAS                              How, mortified!

JACOMO

And is admitted to the sisterhood.                              340

BARABAS

Child of perdition, and thy father's shame,
What wilt thou do among these hateful fiends?
I charge thee on my blessing that thou leave
These devils, and their damnèd heresy.

ABIGAIL

Father give me –

BARABAS                    Nay back, Abigail                              345
(And think upon the jewels and the gold,
The board is marked thus that covers it).

                              [*Makes sign of the cross*]

Away, accursèd from thy father's sight.

JACOMO

Barabas, although thou art in misbelief,
And wilt not see thine own afflictions,                              350
Yet let thy daughter be no longer blind.

BARABAS

Blind, friar? I reck not thy persuasions.
(The board is markèd thus † that covers it.)
For I had rather die, than see her thus.
Wilt thou forsake me too in my distress,                              355
Seducèd daughter? (Go forget not.)
Becomes it Jews to be so credulous?

---

339    *has mortified herself* has died to worldly values
343    *charge* command
345–8   *Nay back . . . sight* Abigail apparently moves toward Barabas, allowing him to whisper
        to her between his two expressions of repulse. Q prints '*Whispers to her*' opposite line
        346.
347    *thus* A standard Elizabethan indication of stage business; the text prints a cross-like
        dagger at 'thus' in line 353.
350    *wilt not see* The Friar attributes Barabas's Jewish faith to his wilfully obstinate
        spiritual blindness.
352    *Blind, friar?* ed. (Q Blind, Fryer,)
        *reck not* pay no heed to
353–61  Q prints lines 353, 358, 361 and portions of line 356 in italics. Next to lines 356
        and 358 '*aside to her*' appears in the margin.
356    *Seducèd daughter?* ed. (Q Seduced Daughter,)
357    *credulous?* ed. (Q credulous,)

(Tomorrow early I'll be at the door.)
No come not at me, if thou wilt be damned,
Forget me, see me not, and so be gone.                                    360
(Farewell. Remember tomorrow morning.)
Out, out thou wretch.

[*Exeunt:* BARABAS *on one side;*
FRIARS, ABBESS, NUN, *and* ABIGAIL *on the other*]

*Enter* MATHIAS

MATHIAS
Who's this? Fair Abigail the rich Jew's daughter
Become a nun? Her father's sudden fall
Has humbled her and brought her down to this:                              365
Tut, she were fitter for a tale of love
Than to be tirèd out with orisons:
And better would she far become a bed
Embracèd in a friendly lover's arms,
Than rise at midnight to a solemn mass.                                    370

*Enter* LODOWICK

LODOWICK
Why how now Don Mathias, in a dump?
MATHIAS
Believe me, noble Lodowick, I have seen
The strangest sight, in my opinion,
That ever I beheld.
LODOWICK                      What was't, I prithee?
MATHIAS
A fair young maid scarce fourteen years of age,                           375
The sweetest flower in Cytherea's field,
Cropped from the pleasures of the fruitful earth,
And strangely metamorphosed nun.
LODOWICK
But say, what was she?
MATHIAS                      Why the rich Jew's daughter.

364    *Become a nun? Her* ed. (Q Become a Nun, her)
367    *orisons* prayers
371    *in a dump* in a state of gloom
374    *was't, I* ed. (Q wast I)
376    *Cytherea* Venus
378    *metamorphosed nun* transformed to a nun. Many editions add to this line to make
       it read: 'And strangely metamorphosed to a nun'.

LODOWICK
    What Barabas, whose goods were lately seized?         380
    Is she so fair?
MATHIAS         And matchless beautiful;
    As had you seen her 'twould have moved your heart,
    Though countermured with walls of brass, to love,
    Or at the least to pity.
LODOWICK
    And if she be so fair as you report,         385
    'Twere time well spent to go and visit her:
    How say you, shall we?
MATHIAS
    I must and will, sir, there's no remedy.
LODOWICK
    And so will I too, or it shall go hard.
    Farewell Mathias.
MATHIAS         Farewell Lodowick.         390

                               *Exeunt*

383   *countermured* ed. (Q countermin'd) fortified with a double wall
385   *And if* If
388   *remedy* alternative
389   *or it shall go hard* come what may

# ACT II [SCENE i]

*Enter* BARABAS *with a light*

BARABAS

Thus like the sad presaging raven that tolls
The sick man's passport in her hollow beak,
And in the shadow of the silent night
Doth shake contagion from her sable wings,
Vexed and tormented runs poor Barabas                          5
With fatal curses towards these Christians.
The incertain pleasures of swift-footed time
Have ta'en their flight, and left me in despair;
And of my former riches rests no more
But bare remembrance; like a soldier's scar,                  10
That has no further comfort for his maim.
Oh thou that with a fiery pillar led'st
The sons of Israel through the dismal shades,
Light Abraham's offspring; and direct the hand
Of Abigail this night; or let the day                         15
Turn to eternal darkness after this:
No sleep can fasten on my watchful eyes,
Nor quiet enter my distempered thoughts,
Till I have answer of my Abigail.

*Enter* ABIGAIL *above*

ABIGAIL

Now have I happily espied a time                              20
To search the plank my father did appoint;

---

1       *presaging ... tolls* foreboding ... announces
2       *passport* i.e. allowing entry to death's kingdom
4       *wings,* ed. (Q wings;)
9       *rests* remains
11      *maim* wound
12–13   See Exodus 13.21–2.
18      *distempered* agitated
20–2    *Now ... here, behold, unseen,* ed. (Q (unseen)) Abigail, l ke her father in being unaware
        that anyone else is on-stage, is represented as discovering the treasure as she speaks.
        *appoint* designate

And here behold, unseen, where I have found
The gold, the pearls, and jewels which he hid.

BARABAS

Now I remember those old women's words,
Who in my wealth would tell me winter's tales,                    25
And speak of spirits and ghosts that glide by night
About the place where treasure hath been hid:
And now methinks that I am one of those:
For whilst I live, here lives my soul's sole hope,
And when I die, here shall my spirit walk.                        30

ABIGAIL

Now that my father's fortune were so good
As but to be about this happy place;
'Tis not so happy: yet when we parted last,
He said he would attend me in the morn.
Then, gentle sleep, where'er his body rests,                      35
Give charge to Morpheus that he may dream
A golden dream, and of the sudden walk,
Come and receive the treasure I have found.

BARABAS

*Bien para todos mi ganada no es:*
As good go on, as sit so sadly thus.                             40
But stay, what star shines yonder in the east?
The loadstar of my life, if Abigail.
Who's there?

ABIGAIL                    Who's that?

BARABAS                                    Peace, Abigail, 'tis I.

ABIGAIL

Then father here receive thy happiness.

BARABAS

Hast thou't?                          [ABIGAIL] *Throws down bags*    45

---

25    *wealth* time of prosperity
      *winter's tales* fanciful stories
31    *Now that* Now if only
36    *Morpheus* son of sleep and god of dreams (compare Ovid, *Metamorphoses* XI.623ff)
37    *walk* often amended to 'wake,' but possibly meaning 'arise' or 'sleepwalk'
39    *Bien para todos mi ganada no es:* ed. (Q *Birn para todos, my ganada no er:*) (Spanish)
      My gain is not good for everybody
42    *loadstar* guiding star

ABIGAIL

    Here,

    Hast thou't?

    There's more, and more, and more.

BARABAS                      Oh my girl,

    My gold, my fortune, my felicity;

    Strength to my soul, death to mine enemy;         50

    Welcome the first beginner of my bliss:

    Oh Abigail, Abigail, that I had thee here too,

    Then my desires were fully satisfied.

    But I will practise thy enlargement thence:

    Oh girl, oh gold, oh beauty, oh my bliss!     *Hugs his bags*   55

ABIGAIL

    Father, it draweth towards midnight now,

    And 'bout this time the nuns begin to wake;

    To shun suspicion, therefore, let us part.

BARABAS

    Farewell my joy, and by my fingers take

    A kiss from him that sends it from his soul.         60

    Now Phoebus ope the eye-lids of the day,

    And for the raven wake the morning lark,

    That I may hover with her in the air,

    Singing o'er these, as she does o'er her young.

    *Hermoso placer de los dineros.*              65

                                  *Exeunt*

---

46–8   *Here . . . more, and more, and more* The short lines and repetitions may suggest repeated action of throwing down the bags.

54   *practise thy enlargement* contrive your release

61   *Phoebus* Apollo, god of light and the sun

62   *for* in place of

65   *Hermoso placer de los dineros* ed. (Q *Hermoso piarer, de les Denirch*) (Spanish) beautiful pleasure of money

# [ACT II, SCENE ii]

*Enter* GOVERNOR [FERNEZE], MARTIN DEL BOSCO,
*the* KNIGHTS [*and* OFFICERS]

FERNEZE

    Now Captain tell us whither thou art bound?

    Whence is thy ship that anchors in our road?

    And why thou cam'st ashore without our leave?

BOSCO

    Governor of Malta, hither am I bound;

    My ship, the Flying Dragon, is of Spain,                 5

    And so am I, Del Bosco is my name;

    Vice-admiral unto the Catholic king.

1 KNIGHT

    'Tis true, my lord, therefore entreat him well.

BOSCO

    Our fraught is Grecians, Turks, and Afric Moors,

    For late upon the coast of Corsica,                 10

    Because we vailed not to the Turkish fleet,

    Their creeping galleys had us in the chase:

    But suddenly the wind began to rise,

    And then we luffed and tacked, and fought at ease:

    Some have we fired, and many have we sunk;        15

    But one amongst the rest became our prize:

    The captain's slaine, the rest remain our slaves,

    Of whom we would make sale in Malta here.

FERNEZE

    Martin del Bosco, I have heard of thee;

    Welcome to Malta, and to all of us;              20

  1   *FERNEZE* Q calls Ferneze 'Governor' throughout the scene.
  2   *Whence* From where
  7   *Catholic king* according to Bawcutt a traditional title of the king of Spain
  8   *entreat* treat
  9   *fraught* cargo
 11   *vailed* lowered sails in token of respect
      *Turkish* ed. (Q Spanish)
 12   *creeping* slow
 14   *luffed and tacked* ed. (Q left, and tooke) turned our ship into the wind and sailed
      obliquely against it
 15   *fired* burned

But to admit a sale of these thy Turks
We may not, nay we dare not give consent
By reason of a tributary league.

1 KNIGHT

Del Bosco, as thou lovest and honour'st us,
Persuade our Governor against the Turk;                    25
This truce we have is but in hope of gold,
And with that sum he craves might we wage war.

BOSCO

Will Knights of Malta be in league with Turks,
And buy it basely too for sums of gold?
My lord, remember that to Europe's shame,                  30
The Christian isle of Rhodes, from whence you came,
Was lately lost, and you were stated here
To be at deadly enmity with Turks.

FERNEZE

Captain we know it, but our force is small.

BOSCO

What is the sum that Calymath requires?                    35

FERNEZE

A hundred thousand crowns.

BOSCO

My lord and king hath title to this isle,
And he means quickly to expel them hence;
Therefore be ruled by me, and keep the gold:
I'll write unto his Majesty for aid,                       40
And not depart until I see you free.

FERNEZE

On this condition shall thy Turks be sold.
Go officers and set them straight in show.

[*Exeunt* OFFICERS]

23    *tributary league* an alliance involving monetary payment
27    *he* the Turk
32    *lately lost* Rhodes fell to the Turks in 1522; in 1530 Malta was granted to the Knights
      by Charles V.
      *stated* installed in office
38    *them* ed. (Q you) Editors have assumed a confusion of pronouns here like the
      confusion of enemies in line 11; however, as Bawcutt argues, it is possible that the
      uncertainty is authorial. A multiple and evolving sense of who is the enemy of whom
      would fit with Emily Bartels's account of the play in terms of imperialism ('Malta,
      the Jew, and the Fictions of Difference: Colonialist Discourse in Marlowe's *Jew of
      Malta*', *ELR* 20 (1990), 3–16).

Bosco, thou shalt be Malta's general;
We and our warlike knights will follow thee                    45
Against these barbarous misbelieving Turks.

BOSCO

So shall you imitate those you succeed:
For when their hideous force environed Rhodes,
Small though the number was that kept the town,
They fought it out, and not a man survived              50
To bring the hapless news to Christendom.

FERNEZE

So will we fight it out; come let's away:
Proud-daring Calymath, instead of gold,
We'll send thee bullets wrapped in smoke and fire:
Claim tribute where thou wilt, we are resolved,           55
Honour is bought with blood and not with gold.

*Exeunt*

---

46    *misbelieving* non-Christian
47–51  *So . . . Christendom.* The siege of Rhodes in 1522 did not result in the total destruc-
       tion Del Bosco claims.
51    *hapless* unfortunate
54    *send thee* ed. (Q send the)

# [ACT II, SCENE iii]

*Enter* OFFICERS *with* [ITHAMORE *and other*] SLAVES

1 OFFICER

    This is the market-place, here let 'em stand:
    Fear not their sale, for they'll be quickly bought.

2 OFFICER

    Every one's price is written on his back,
    And so much must they yield or not be sold.

*Enter* BARABAS

1 OFFICER

    Here comes the Jew, had not his goods been seized,        5
    He'd give us present money for them all.

BARABAS

    In spite of these swine-eating Christians,
    Unchosen nation, never circumcised;
    Such as, poor villains, were ne'er thought upon
    Till Titus and Vespasian conquered us,        10
    Am I become as wealthy as I was:
    They hoped my daughter would ha' been a nun;
    But she's at home, and I have bought a house
    As great and fair as is the Governor's;
    And there in spite of Malta will I dwell:        15
    Having Ferneze's hand, whose heart I'll have;
    Ay, and his son's too, or it shall go hard.

---

   4   s.d. Q has entry directions for Barabas here and at line 7.
   6   *present money* ready cash
   8   *Unchosen nation* Referring to the idea of the Jews as God's chosen people
8–10   ed. (Q (Vnchosen . . . circumciz'd; / Such . . . vpon / Till . . . vs.))
   9   *Such as, poor villains,* ed. (Q Such as poore villaines)
       *villains* low fellows
       *ne'er thought upon* disregarded
 10   *Titus and Vespasian* Vespasian and his son Titus, successive Roman Emperors, led the campaigns that resulted in the fall of Jerusalem in A.D. 70.
 16   *Ferneze's hand* either Ferneze's written assurance of safety or his handshake in friendship
 17   *go hard* be unfortunate

44

I am not of the tribe of Levi, I,
That can so soon forget an injury.
We Jews can fawn like spaniels when we please;                    20
And when we grin we bite, yet are our looks
As innocent and harmless as a lamb's.
I learned in Florence how to kiss my hand,
Heave up my shoulders when they call me dog,
And duck as low as any bare-foot friar,                          25
Hoping to see them starve upon a stall,
Or else be gathered for in our synagogue;
That when the offering-basin comes to me,
Even for charity I may spit into't.
Here comes Don Lodowick the Governor's son,                       30
One that I love for his good father's sake.

*Enter* LODOWICK

LODOWICK

I hear the wealthy Jew walked this way;
I'll seek him out, and so insinuate,
That I may have a sight of Abigail;
For Don Mathias tells me she is fair.                             35

BARABAS

(Now will I show myself to have more of the serpent than the
dove; that is, more knave than fool.)

LODOWICK

Yond walks the Jew, now for fair Abigail.

BARABAS

(Ay, ay, no doubt but she's at your command.)

---

18    *tribe of Levi* the tribe associated with priestliness and jurisdiction over the cities of
      refuge (Joshua 20–1)
20    *fawn* affect a servile fondness
21    *grin* smile
24    *Heave up* Shrug
25    *duck* bow humbly (see III.iii.51)
26    *stall* a commercial display platform sometimes used for a bed by impoverished
      vagrants
27    *be gathered for* have a collection taken for them
33    *insinuate* work myself into favour
36–7  ed. (Q Now ... serpent / Then ... foole.)
      *more of the serpent than the dove* more cunning than innocence (twisting the admo-
      nition of Matthew 10.16: 'be ye therefore wise as serpentes, and innocent as doues')

LODOWICK

    Barabas, thou know'st I am the Governor's son.        40

BARABAS

    I would you were his father too, sir, that's all the harm I wish
    you. (The slave looks like a hog's cheek new singed.)

                              [BARABAS *turns away*]

LODOWICK

    Whither walk'st thou Barabas?

BARABAS

    No further: 'tis a custom held with us,
    That when we speak with Gentiles like to you,        45
    We turn into the air to purge ourselves:
    For unto us the promise doth belong.

LODOWICK

    Well, Barabas, canst help me to a diamond?

BARABAS

    Oh, sir, your father had my diamonds.
    Yet I have one left that will serve your turn:        50
    I mean my daughter. (But ere he shall have her
    I'll sacrifice her on a pile of wood.
    I ha' the poison of the city for him,
    And the white leprosy.)

LODOWICK

    What sparkle does it give without a foil?`        55

BARABAS

    The diamond that I talk of, ne'er was foiled
    (But when he touches it, it will be foiled).

---

41–2    ed. (Q 1 . . . harm / I wish you . . . new sindg'd.) Unclear in meaning.

42    *hog's cheek new singed* i.e. Lodowick is recently shaven

47    *the promise* See I.i.104–5n.

51    ed. (Q 1 mean my daughter: – but . . . ) Q prints 'aside' opposite line 52, but the dash
       in the Q version of line 51 may indicate the beginning of the aside (as apparently in
       lines 60 and 67). However, as Craik points out, 'I mean my daughter' may be an aside,
       since Lodowick and Barabas 'continue talking of Abigail obliquely as a diamond'.

53–4    ed. (Q the / White)

53    *poison of the city* . . . *white leprosy* not satisfactorily explained but apparently refer-
       ences to a virulent poison and a natural disease associated with cities, such as the
       plague

55    *foil* thin metallic leaf set under a gem to add to its brilliance

56    *foiled* set by a jeweller

57    ed. (Q But . . . foiled:)
       *foiled* defiled, dishonoured

Lord Lodowick, it sparkles bright and fair.

LODOWICK

Is it square or pointed? Pray let me know.

BARABAS

Pointed it is, good sir (but not for you).                    60

LODOWICK

I like it much the better.

BARABAS                                    So do I too.

LODOWICK

How shows it by night?

BARABAS                           Outshines Cynthia's rays:

You'll like it better far a' nights than days.

LODOWICK

And what's the price?

BARABAS

(Your life and if you have it.) O my lord                    65

We will not jar about the price; come to my house

And I will give't your honour (with a vengeance).

LODOWICK

No, Barabas, I will deserve it first.

BARABAS

Good sir,

Your father has deserved it at my hands,                    70

Who of mere charity and Christian ruth,

To bring me to religious purity,

And as it were in catechizing sort,

To make me mindful of my mortal sins,

Against my will, and whether I would or no,                    75

Seized all I had, and thrust me out-a-doors,

---

    59   ed. (Q pointed,)

  59–60  *pointed* denoting the cut of a gem, but used by Barabas to mean 'appointed' or
       'promised'

    60   ed. (Q Pointed it is, good Sir, – but not for you.) Q has an '*aside*' in the margin.

    62   *Cynthia* the moon

    63   Q marks the line '*aside*'; Craik suggests this may refer to line 65.

    65   ed. (Q Your life and if you haue it. – Oh my Lord)

       *and if* if

    66   *jar* quarrel

    67   ed. (Q And I will giu't your honour – with a vengeance.) Line 67 is marked '*aside*' in Q.

  69–70  ed. (Q *one line*)

    71   *ruth* pity

    73   *in catechizing sort* in the manner of religious instruction

And made my house a place for nuns most chaste.
LODOWICK
No doubt your soul shall reap the fruit of it.
BARABAS
Ay, but my lord, the harvest is far off:
And yet I know the prayers of those nuns                    80
And holy friars, having money for their pains,
Are wondrous; (and indeed do no man good)
And seeing they are not idle, but still doing,
'Tis likely they in time may reap some fruit,
I mean in fullness of perfection.                           85
LODOWICK
Good Barabas glance not at our holy nuns.
BARABAS
No, but I do it through a burning zeal
(Hoping ere long to set the house afire;
For though they do awhile increase and multiply,
I'll have a saying to that nunnery).                        90
As for the diamond, sir, I told you of,
Come home and there's no price shall make us part,
Even for your honourable father's sake.
(It shall go hard but I will see your death.)
But now I must be gone to buy a slave.                      95
LODOWICK
And, Barabas, I'll bear thee company.
BARABAS
Come then, here's the marketplace; what's the price of this slave,

---

82    ed. (Q Are wondrous; *and indeed doe no man good:*) This line is also marked with a
      marginal '*aside*' Line 86 suggests that Lodowick hears the remainder of Barabas's
      speech.
83–5  *still doing* always copulating
      *still doing . . . perfection* Barabas employs the terms of Lodowick's theological dis-
      course to suggest the hypocrisy of the nuns' and friars' claims to chastity.
86    *glance not* do not criticize by innuendo
88–90 italicized in Q with marginal '*aside*' opposite line 89
89    *increase and multiply* The nuns, while professing chastity, fulfil God's command to
      Noah (Genesis 9).
90    *have a saying to* have something to say about
94    italicized in Q with marginal '*aside*'
      *It shall go hard but* Unless prevented by the power of circumstances it will happen that
97–8  ed. (Q Come . . . price / Of . . . much?)

two hundred crowns? Do the Turks weigh so much?

1 OFFICER

Sir, that's his price.

BARABAS

What, can he steal that you demand so much?                    100
Belike he has some new trick for a purse;
And if he has, he is worth three hundred plates,
So that, being bought, the town seal might be got
To keep him for his lifetime from the gallows.
The sessions day is critical to thieves,                          105
And few or none 'scape but by being purged.

LODOWICK

Ratest thou this Moor but at two hundred plates?

1 OFFICER

No more, my lord.

BARABAS

Why should this Turk be dearer than that Moor?

1 OFFICER

Because he is young and has more qualities.                     110

BARABAS

What, hast the philosopher's stone? And thou hast, break my
head with it, I'll forgive thee.

SLAVE

No sir, I can cut and shave.

BARABAS

Let me see, sirrah, are you not an old shaver?

SLAVE

Alas, sir, I am a very youth.                                     115

---

   98   *Turks* ed. (Q *Turke*)
  102   *plates,* ed. (Q *plats.*) silver coins
102–6   *And if . . . purged* He might be worth so much as a thief if one could get governmental
        assurance of pardon; trial days are fatal to thieves, few escaping the 'cure' of being
        hanged
  110   *qualities* abilities
111–12  ed. (Q *What . . . hast, / Breake . . . thee.*)
  111   *philosopher's stone* the much sought-after goal of alchemy, a stone that would turn
        other metals to gold
        *And* if
113–22  *SLAVE* ed. (Q *Itha.* or *Ith.*)
  114   *old shaver* rogue, rascal
  115   *very* genuine

BARABAS

A youth? I'll buy you, and marry you to Lady Vanity if you
do well.

SLAVE

I will serve you, sir.

BARABAS

Some wicked trick or other. It may be under colour of shaving,
thou'lt cut my throat for my goods. Tell me, hast thou thy     120
health well?

SLAVE

Ay, passing well.

BARABAS

So much the worse; I must have one that's sickly, and't be but
for sparing vittles: 'tis not a stone of beef a day will maintain
you in these chops; let me see one that's somewhat leaner.     125

1 OFFICER

Here's a leaner, how like you him?

BARABAS

Where wast thou born?

ITHAMORE

In Thrace; brought up in Arabia.

BARABAS

So much the better, thou art for my turn;
An hundred crowns, I'll have him; there's the coin.     130

[*Pays money*]

1 OFFICER

Then mark him, sir, and take him hence.

BARABAS

(Ay, mark him, you were best, for this is he
That by my help shall do much villainy.)

116–17   ed. (Q A ... vanity / If ... well.) *Youth* and *Vanity* are stock figures of the morality
         plays; as Craik observes, Barabas's promise to marry Youth to Vanity would encour-
         age vice rather than virtue.
119–21   ed. (Q Some ... colour / Of ... goods. / Tell ... well?)
   119   *colour* pretence
123–5   ed. (Q So ... sickly, / And ... day / Will ... one / That's ... leaner.)
123–4   *and't be but for* ed. (Q And be but for) if only for the sake of
   124   *stone* fourteen pounds
   125   *chops* jowls
   127   *wast* ed. (Q was)
   128   *Thrace* ed. (Q Trace)
   129   *for my turn;* ed. (Q for my turn,) suited for my purposes
   132   *mark* observe, pay attention to

50

My lord farewell: [*To* ITHAMORE] come sirrah you are mine.
[*To* LODOWICK] As for the diamond, it shall be yours;       135
I pray, sir, be no stranger at my house,
All that I have shall be at your command.

      *Enter* MATHIAS [*and his*] MOTHER [KATHERINE]

MATHIAS
  (What makes the Jew and Lodowick so private?
  I fear me 'tis about fair Abigail.)
BARABAS
  Yonder comes Don Mathias, let us stay;       140
  He loves my daughter, and she holds him dear:
  But I have sworn to frustrate both their hopes,
  And be revenged upon the – (Governor).
                    [*Exit* LODOWICK]

KATHERINE
  This Moor is comeliest, is he not? Speak, son.
MATHIAS
  No, this is the better, mother, view this well.       145
BARABAS
  (Seem not to know me here before your mother,
  Lest she mistrust the match that is in hand:
  When you have brought her home, come to my house;
  Think of me as thy father; son farewell.
MATHIAS
  But wherefore talked Don Lodowick with you?       150
BARABAS
  Tush man, we talked of diamonds, not of Abigail.)
KATHERINE
  Tell me, Mathias, is not that the Jew?
BARABAS
  As for the comment on the Maccabees,

---

137    s.d. ed. (Q *Enter Mathias, Mater;* her speeches so headed throughout)
140    *let us stay* let us break off our talk
141–3  The addressee of these lines is difficult to determine. Q's punctuation of line 143
      (And be reveng'd upon the – Governor) is typical of its treatment of Barabas's asides
      at the end of lines, and this suggests that he addresses most of the speech to Lodo-
      wick; but, as Bawcutt points out, at line 284 Lodowick appears unaware of Abigail's
      love for Mathias, so perhaps he exits as Mathias enters.
147    *mistrust* suspect
153    *comment on the Maccabees* commentary on the two apocryphal biblical books of
      the Maccabees

I have it, sir, and 'tis at your command.

MATHIAS

Yes, madam, and my talk with him was                                    155
About the borrowing of a book or two.

KATHERINE

Converse not with him, he is cast off from heaven.

[*To* OFFICER] Thou hast thy crowns, fellow, [*To* MATHIAS]
    come let's away.

MATHIAS

Sirrah, Jew, remember the book.

BARABAS

Marry will I, sir.                                                      160

                    *Exeunt* [MATHIAS *and* MOTHER *with* SLAVE]

1 OFFICER

Come, I have made a reasonable market, let's away.

                            [*Exeunt* OFFICERS *with* SLAVES]

BARABAS

Now let me know thy name, and therewithal
Thy birth, condition, and profession.

ITHAMORE

Faith, sir, my birth is but mean, my name's Ithamore, my profession what you please.                                                165

BARABAS

Hast thou no trade? Then listen to my words,
And I will teach that shall stick by thee:
First be thou void of these affections,
Compassion, love, vain hope, and heartless fear,
Be moved at nothing, see thou pity none,                               170
But to thyself smile when the Christians moan.

ITHAMORE

Oh brave, master, I worship your nose for this.

BARABAS

As for myself, I walk abroad a-nights
And kill sick people groaning under walls:

160   s.d. (Q places after line 158)
163   *condition* social standing
164   *mean* low
167   *stick by thee* be worth remembering
168   *affections* feelings
169   *heartless* cowardly
172   *brave* wonderful
      *your nose* alluding to Barabas's huge nose (see III.iii.9–10)

Sometimes I go about and poison wells; 175
And now and then, to cherish Christian thieves,
I am content to lose some of my crowns;
That I may, walking in my gallery,
See 'em go pinioned along by my door.
Being young I studied physic, and began 180
To practise first upon the Italian;
There I enriched the priests with burials,
And always kept the sexton's arms in ure
With digging graves and ringing dead men's knells:
And after that was I an engineer, 185
And in the wars 'twixt France and Germany,
Under pretence of helping Charles the Fifth,
Slew friend and enemy with my stratagems.
Then after that was I an usurer, *cheating*
And with extorting, cozening, forfeiting, 190
And tricks belonging unto brokery,
I filled the jails with bankrouts in a year,
And with young orphans planted hospitals,
And every moon made some or other mad,
And now and then one hang himself for grief, 195
Pinning upon his breast a long great scroll
How I with interest tormented him.
But mark how I am blest for plaguing them,
I have as much coin as will buy the town.
But tell me now, how hast thou spent thy time? 200

ITHAMORE

Faith, master,
In setting Christian villages on fire,

178    *gallery* balcony (see V.v.33)
179    *pinioned* with arms tied together
180    *physic* medicine
183    *ure* use
185    *engineer* builder of military engines
186–7  Struggles betwen the forces of the Holy Roman Emperor, Charles V (1500–58), and
       the French king, Francis I, continued between 1519 and 1558.
189    *usurer* money-lender; usually associated with high rates (compare IV.i.54)
190    *cozening* cheating
       *forfeiting* profiting from the failure of borrowers to repay their loans
191    *brokery* dishonest financial transactions
192    *bankrouts* bankrupts
193    *planted* furnished        *hospitals* charitable institutions, almshouses
201–2  ed. (Q *one line*)

Chaining of eunuchs, binding galley-slaves.
One time I was an hostler in an inn,
And in the night time secretly would I steal                                    205
To travellers' chambers, and there cut their throats:
Once at Jerusalem, where the pilgrims kneeled,
I strowèd powder on the marble stones,
And therewithal their knees would rankle, so
That I have laughed a-good to see the cripples                                  210
Go limping home to Christendom on stilts.

BARABAS

Why this is something: make account of me
As of thy fellow; we are villains both:
Both circumcisèd, we hate Christians both:
Be true and secret, thou shalt want no gold.                                    215
But stand aside, here comes Don Lodowick.

*Enter* LODOWICK

LODOWICK

Oh Barabas well met;
Where is the diamond you told me of?

BARABAS

I have it for you, sir; please you walk in with me:
What, ho, Abigail; open the door I say.                                         220

*Enter* ABIGAIL

ABIGAIL

In good time, father, here are letters come
From Ormus, and the post stays here within.

BARABAS

Give me the letters, daughter, do you hear?
Entertain Lodowick the Governor's son

204    *hostler* stable keeper
209    *rankle* fester
210    *a-good* heartily
211    *stilts* crutches
212    *make account of me* think of me
215    *want* lack
217–18  ed. (Q Oh . . . Diamond / You . . . of?)
221    *In good time* Just in time
222    *Ormus* town on the Persian Gulf, known in the Renaissance for trading in luxuries
       *post* messenger
223–9  This edition follows Q, which has '*aside*' opposite line 227 and prints the word
       'Philistine' and lines 228–9 in italics. As Craik points out, it is typical of Barabas to

With all the courtesy you can afford;                    225
Provided, that you keep your maidenhead.
Use him as if he were a (Philistine.
Dissemble, swear, protest, vow to love him,
He is not of the seed of Abraham.)
I am a little busy, sir, pray pardon me.                 230
Abigail, bid him welcome for my sake.

ABIGAIL
For your sake and his own he's welcome hither.

BARABAS
Daughter, a word more. (Kiss him, speak him fair,
And like a cunning Jew so cast about,
That ye be both made sure ere you come out.            235

ABIGAIL
Oh father, Don Mathias is my love.

BARABAS
I know it: yet I say make love to him;
Do, it is requisite it should be so.)
Nay on my life it is my factor's hand,
But go you in, I'll think upon the account:            240

        [*Exeunt* LODOWICK *and* ABIGAIL]

The account is made, for Lodowick dies.
My factor sends me word a merchant's fled
That owes me for a hundred tun of wine:
I weigh it thus much; I have wealth enough.
For now by this has he kissed Abigail;                  245
And she vows love to him, and he to her.
As sure as heaven rained manna for the Jews,

employ final words to reverse the sense of phrases; the advice to Abigail in line 226, as Bawcutt observes, may be a coarse joke intended for Lodowick's appreciation. Q's comma after 'Provided' may suggest a slightly retarded ponderous pace, potentially indicative of self-irony.

227   *Philistine* biblical enemies of the Jews
229   *seed* offspring
233   ed. (Q Daughter, a word more; kisse him, speake him faire,)
234   *cast about* devise
235   *made sure* betrothed
239   *factor's hand* agent's handwriting
240   *account* financial reckoning, with a play on the next line's meaning of 'settling scores'
243   *tun* barrel
244   *thus much* Barabas probably makes a dismissive gesture.
245   *by this* by this time
247   *manna* food given the Jews by heaven (see Exodus 16)

So sure shall he and Don Mathias die:
His father was my chiefest enemy.

*Enter* MATHIAS

Whither goes Don Mathias? Stay a while.                                    250
MATHIAS
Whither but to my fair love Abigail?
BARABAS
Thou know'st, and heaven can witness it is true,
That I intend my daughter shall be thine.
MATHIAS
Ay, Barabas, or else thou wrong'st me much.
BARABAS
Oh heaven forbid I should have such a thought.                              255
Pardon me though I weep; the Governor's son
Will, whether I will or no, have Abigail:
He sends her letters, bracelets, jewels, rings.
MATHIAS
Does she receive them?
BARABAS
She? No, Mathias, no, but sends them back,                                  260
And when he comes, she locks herself up fast;
Yet through the keyhole will he talk to her,
While she runs to the window looking out
When you should come and hale him from the door.
MATHIAS
Oh treacherous Lodowick!                                                    265
BARABAS
Even now as I came home, he slipped me in,
And I am sure he is with Abigail.
MATHIAS
I'll rouse him thence.                                    [*Draws a sword*]
BARABAS
Not for all Malta, therefore sheathe your sword;
If you love me, no quarrels in my house;                                    270

---

249    *was* i.e. in the seizure of his property
       s.d. follows 250 in Q
261    *fast* securely
264    *hale* pull violently
266    *slipped me in* slipped in
268    *rouse* drive from concealment (as a hunter's quarry)

But steal you in, and seem to see him not;
I'll give him such a warning ere he goes
As he shall have small hopes of Abigail.
Away, for here they come.

*Enter* LODOWICK, ABIGAIL

MATHIAS
What hand in hand, I cannot suffer this.                      275
BARABAS
Mathias, as thou lov'st me, not a word.
MATHIAS
Well, let it pass, another time shall serve.          *Exit*
LODOWICK
Barabas, is not that the widow's son?
BARABAS
Ay, and take heed, for he hath sworn your death.
LODOWICK
My death? What is the base-born peasant mad?                  280
BARABAS
No, no, but happily he stands in fear
Of that which you, I think, ne'er dream upon,
My daughter here, a paltry silly girl.
LODOWICK
Why, loves she Don Mathias?
BARABAS
Doth she not with her smiling answer you?                     285
ABIGAIL
(He has my heart, I smile against my will.)
LODOWICK
Barabas, thou know'st I have loved thy daughter long.
BARABAS
And so has she done you, even from a child.

275   *suffer* endure
281   *happily* perhaps
281–3  Whatever the exact sense of these lines, it appears that Barabas means to elicit a
       declaration of love by insinuating that Mathias takes Abigail more seriously than
       does Lodowick.
283   *silly* unsophisticated
284   *Why, loves* ed. (Q Why loves)
288   *even from a child* ever since childhood

LODOWICK

And now I can no longer hold my mind.

BARABAS

Nor I the affection that I bear to you. 290

LODOWICK

This is thy diamond, tell me, shall I have it?

BARABAS

Win it and wear it, it is yet unsoiled.
Oh but I know your lordship would disdain
To marry with the daughter of a Jew:
And yet I'll give her many a golden cross 295
With Christian posies round about the ring.

LODOWICK

'Tis not thy wealth, but her that I esteem,
Yet crave I thy consent.

BARABAS

And mine you have, yet let me talk to her.
(This offspring of Cain, this Jebusite 300
That never tasted of the Passover,
Nor e'er shall see the land of Canaan,
Nor our Messias that is yet to come,
This gentle maggot Lodowick I mean,
Must be deluded: let him have thy hand, 305
But keep thy heart till Don Mathias comes.

ABIGAIL

What shall I be betrothed to Lodowick?

289    *hold my mind* conceal my feelings
292    *unsoiled* undefiled, virginal
295    *cross* coin stamped with a cross
296    *Christian posies* pious mottoes to be found both on coins of the period and on
       wedding rings
299    ed. (Q And ... her;)
300–312    *aside* opposite line 303 in Q
300    *offspring of Cain* a degenerate race in Jewish and Christian traditions, descended
       from the first biblical murderer
       *Jebusite* member of the original Canaanite tribe driven from Jerusalem by King
       David (see II Samuel 5)
301    *Passover* the important Jewish ritual, commemorating the deliverance from Egypt
       described in Exodus 12
302    *Canaan* the land promised the Jews in Genesis 17
303    *Messias* Messiah
304    *gentle maggot* punning on 'gentle' as 'gentleman', as 'gentile', and as a synonym for
       'maggot'

BARABAS

It's no sin to deceive a Christian;
For they themselves hold it a principle,
Faith is not to be held with heretics;
But all are heretics that are not Jews; 310
This follows well, and therefore daughter fear not.)
I have entreated her, and she will grant.

LODOWICK

Then gentle Abigail plight thy faith to me.

ABIGAIL

I cannot choose, seeing my father bids: 315
Nothing but death shall part my love and me.

LODOWICK

Now have I that for which my soul hath longed.

BARABAS

(So have not I, but yet I hope I shall.)

ABIGAIL

(Oh wretched Abigail, what hast thou done?)

LODOWICK

Why on the sudden is your colour changed? 320

ABIGAIL

I know not, but farewell, I must be gone.

BARABAS

Stay her, but let her not speak one word more.

LODOWICK

Mute o' the sudden; here's a sudden change.

BARABAS

Oh muse not at it, 'tis the Hebrews' guise,
That maidens new betrothed should weep a while: 325

308–10  This doctrine is a favourite object of Protestant polemic, which associated it with
        Catholic treachery as exemplified by the Council of Constance (1415) in its justi-
        fication of action against Jan Hus despite an agreement of safe-conduct. See
        2 *Tamburlaine* II.i.
   312  *This follows well* this is good logic
   314  *plight thy faith* enter into a binding betrothal, promising to marry
315–16  Line 315 may be audible to Lodowick, since it could be understood to represent a
        traditional view of a daughter's obligation rather than mere constraint; Abigail
        equivocates in line 316, since 'my love' could be taken by Lodowick to refer to him-
        self.
   318  Q prints '*aside*' in the margin.
   322  *Stay her* either an injunction to Mathias to support Abigail in her distressed state or
        an aside to Ithamore commanding him to keep her quiet (see line 361)
   324  *guise* customary manner

Trouble her not, sweet Lodowick depart:
She is thy wife, and thou shalt be mine heir.

LODOWICK

Oh, is't the custom, then I am resolved;
But rather let the brightsome heavens be dim,
And nature's beauty choke with stifling clouds,                    330
Than my fair Abigail should frown on me.
There comes the villain, now I'll be revenged.

*Enter* MATHIAS

BARABAS

Be quiet Lodowick, it is enough
That I have made thee sure to Abigail.

LODOWICK

Well, let him go.                                          *Exit*      335

BARABAS

Well, but for me, as you went in at doors
You had been stabbed, but not a word on't now;
Here must no speeches pass, nor swords be drawn.

MATHIAS

Suffer me, Barabas, but to follow him.

BARABAS

No; so shall I, if any hurt be done,                              340
Be made an accessary of your deeds;
Revenge it on him when you meet him next.

MATHIAS

For this I'll have his heart.

BARABAS

Do so; lo here I give thee Abigail.

MATHIAS

What greater gift can poor Mathias have?                          345
Shall Lodowick rob me of so fair a love?
My life is not so dear as Abigail.

BARABAS

My heart misgives me, that to cross your love,
He's with your mother, therefore after him.

---

328   *resolved* satisfied
329   *rather* ed. (Q rathe)
339   *Suffer* Allow
348   *misgives me* makes me fear
       *cross* hinder, prevent

MATHIAS
    What, is he gone unto my mother?                  350

BARABAS
    Nay, if you will, stay till she comes herself.

MATHIAS
    I cannot stay; for if my mother come,
    She'll die with grief.                   *Exit*

ABIGAIL
    I cannot take my leave of him for tears:
    Father, why have you thus incensed them both?     355

BARABAS
    What's that to thee?

ABIGAIL             I'll make 'em friends again.

BARABAS
    You'll make 'em friends?
    Are there not Jews enow in Malta,
    But thou must dote upon a Christian?

ABIGAIL
    I will have Don Mathias, he is my love.          360

BARABAS
    Yes, you shall have him: go put her in.

ITHAMORE
    Ay, I'll put her in.

                        *[Puts* ABIGAIL *in]*

BARABAS
    Now tell me, Ithamore, how lik'st thou this?

ITHAMORE
    Faith master, I think by this
    You purchase both their lives; is it not so?      365

BARABAS
    True; and it shall be cunningly performed.

ITHAMORE
    Oh, master, that I might have a hand in this.

BARABAS
    Ay, so thou shalt, 'tis thou must do the deed:
    Take this and bear it to Mathias straight,
    And tell him that it comes from Lodowick.      370

357–8   *You'll . . . friends / Are* ed. (Q You'll . . . Iewes / Enow)
       *enow* enough
  361   *put her in* lock her up in the house
  365   *purchase* obtain

ITHAMORE
    'Tis poisoned, is it not?

BARABAS
    No, no, and yet it might be done that way:
    It is a challenge feigned from Lodowick.

ITHAMORE
    Fear not, I'll so set this heart afire, that he shall verily think it
    comes from him.                                       375

BARABAS
    I cannot choose but like thy readiness:
    Yet be not rash, but do it cunningly.

ITHAMORE
    As I behave myself in this, employ me hereafter.

BARABAS
    Away then.

                                   *Exit* [ITHAMORE]

    So, now will I go in to Lodowick,                    380
    And like a cunning spirit feign some lie,
    Till I have set 'em both at enmity.              *Exit*

374–5    ed. (Q Feare . . . he / Shall . . . him.)
  381    *spirit* devil

# ACT III [SCENE i]

*Enter* [BELLAMIRA] *a* COURTESAN

BELLAMIRA
Since this town was besieged, my gain grows cold:
The time has been, that but for one bare night
A hundred ducats have been freely given:
But now against my will I must be chaste.
And yet I know my beauty doth not fail.                    5
From Venice merchants, and from Padua
Were wont to come rare-witted gentlemen,
Scholars I mean, learnèd and liberal;
And now, save Pilia-Borza, comes there none,
And he is very seldom from my house;                       10
And here he comes.

*Enter* PILIA-BORZA

PILIA-BORZA
Hold thee, wench, there's something for thee to spend.
                                        [*Offers bag of money*]
BELLAMIRA
'Tis silver, I disdain it.
PILIA-BORZA
Ay, but the Jew has gold,
And I will have it or it shall go hard.                    15
BELLAMIRA
Tell me, how cam'st thou by this?

---

  0    s.d. *COURTESAN* high class prostitute
  1    *besieged* As Bennett notes, the siege does not truly begin until the defiance of the
       Turks in III.v. There may have been a rearrangement of scenes; or, as Bawcutt
       suggests, the mere presence of the Turkish fleet has effectively blockaded Malta.
       *my . . . cold* my profits have diminished
  2    *bare* single and/or naked
  6    *Venice . . . Padua* respectively, centres of trade and learning
 6–7   *Padua / Were* ed. (Q Padua, / Were)
  8    *liberal* free-spending (with double sense, like 'cold' and 'bare')
  9    *Pilia-Borza* from the Italian for cutpurse or pickpocket
 12    *Hold thee* Here, take this

PILIA-BORZA

Faith, walking the back lanes through the gardens I chanced to
cast mine eye up to the Jew's counting-house, where I saw
some bags of money, and in the night I clambered up with
my hooks, and as I was taking my choice, I heard a rumbling       20
in the house; so I took only this, and run my way: but here's
the Jew's man.

*Enter* ITHAMORE

BELLAMIRA

Hide the bag.

PILIA-BORZA

Look not towards him, let's away: zoons what a looking thou
keep'st, thou'lt betray's anon.                                   25

[*Exeunt* BELLAMIRA *and* PILIA-BORZA]

ITHAMORE

O the sweetest face that ever I beheld! I know she is a courtesan
by her attire: now would I give a hundred of the Jew's crowns
that I had such a concubine.
Well, I have delivered the challenge in such sort,
As meet they will, and fighting die; brave sport.        *Exit*    30

---

17–22   ed. (Q Faith . . . Gardens / I . . . house / Where . . . I / Clamber'd . . . taking / My . . .
        tooke / Onely . . . man.)

   18   *counting-house,* ed. (Q counting-house)
        *counting-house* business office

   20   *hooks* standard item of burglary equipment

 24–5   ed. (Q Looke . . . away: / Zoon's . . . keep'st, / Thou'lt . . . anon.)

   24   *zoons* zounds, a contraction of 'by God's wounds'

 24–5   *looking . . . keep'st* obvious staring you engage in

   25   *anon* immediately

 26–8   ed. (Q O . . . is / A . . . hundred / Of . . . Concubine.)

   27   *attire* apparently a distinctive form of dress, whether the red taffeta worn by some
        English prostitutes or the more elaborate gowns of their notorious Venetian counter-
        parts

   29   *in such sort* in such a form

   30   *brave sport* admirable jest

# [ACT III, SCENE ii]

*Enter* MATHIAS

MATHIAS
  This is the place, now Abigail shall see
  Whether Mathias holds her dear or no.

*Enter* LODOWICK *reading*

[LODOWICK]
  What, dares the villain write in such base terms?
[MATHIAS]
  I did it, and revenge it if thou dar'st.

*Fight. Enter* BARABAS *above*

BARABAS
  Oh bravely fought, and yet they thrust not home.                    5
  Now Lodowick, now Mathias, so;              [*Both fall*]
  So now they have showed themselves to be tall fellows.
[VOICES] *Within*
  Part 'em, part 'em.
BARABAS
  Ay, part 'em now they are dead: farewell, farewell.        *Exit*

*Enter* GOVERNOR [FERNEZE],
MOTHER [KATHERINE], [*with* CITIZENS]

FERNEZE
  What sight is this? My Lodowick slain!                              10
  These arms of mine shall be thy sepulchre.
KATHERINE
  Who is this? My son Mathias slain!

---

3–4   The text is doubtful. Q gives line 3 to Mathias and line 4 to Lodowick. The entrance
      'reading' and his use of the status terms 'villain' and 'base' argue that t is Lodowick who
      reacts to a communication – probably Mathias's reply to Barabas's forged challenge
      ('feigned from Lodowick' (II.iii.373), since Mathias here acknowledges 'I did it'; but
      later Ithamore claims to have also brought a forged challenge to Lodowick (III.iii.
      18–19), so perhaps both Lodowick and Mathias mistake a forgery for Mathias's own
      letter.
5     *home* deeply, mortally
6     *Now . . . now . . . so* The lines suggest the sword strokes.
7     *tall* brave (ironically)

65

FERNEZE
  Oh Lodowick! had'st thou perished by the Turk,
  Wretched Ferneze might have venged thy death.
KATHERINE
  Thy son slew mine, and I'll revenge his death.                    15
FERNEZE
  Look, Katherine, look, thy son gave mine these wounds.
KATHERINE
  O leave to grieve me, I am grieved enough.
FERNEZE ·
  Oh that my sighs could turn to lively breath;
  And these my tears to blood, that he might live.
KATHERINE
  Who made them enemies?                                            20
FERNEZE
  I know not, and that grieves me most of all.
KATHERINE
  My son loved thine.
FERNEZE                      And so did Lodowick him.
KATHERINE
  Lend me that weapon that did kill my son,
  And it shall murder me.
FERNEZE
  Nay Madam stay, that weapon was my son's,                         25
  And on that rather should Ferneze die.
KATHERINE
  Hold, let's enquire the causers of their deaths,
  That we may venge their blood upon their heads.
FERNEZE
  Then take them up, and let them be interred
  Within one sacred monument of stone;                              30
  Upon which altar I will offer up
  My daily sacrifice of sighs and tears,
  And with my prayers pierce impartial heavens,
  Till they [reveal] the causers of our smarts,

17   *leave* cease
18   *lively* life-giving
33   *impartial* indifferent
34   *reveal* Most editors follow Dyce in assuming some such word to be omitted here.
     *smarts* pains, injuries

Which forced their hands divide united hearts:                    35
Come, Katherine, our losses equal are,
Then of true grief let us take equal share.

*Exeunt* [*with the bodies*]

# [ACT III, SCENE iii]

*Enter* ITHAMORE

ITHAMORE
    Why, was there ever seen such villainy,
    So neatly plotted, and so well performed?
    Both held in hand, and flatly both beguiled.

*Enter* ABIGAIL

ABIGAIL
    Why how now Ithamore, why laugh'st thou so?
ITHAMORE
    Oh, mistress, ha ha ha.                5
ABIGAIL
    Why what ail'st thou?
ITHAMORE
    Oh my master.
ABIGAIL
    Ha.
ITHAMORE
    Oh mistress! I have the bravest, gravest, secret, subtle, bottle-
    nosed knave to my master, that ever gentleman had.     10
ABIGAIL
    Say, knave, why rail'st upon my father thus?
ITHAMORE
    Oh, my master has the bravest policy.
ABIGAIL
    Wherein?

---

  1–3   ed. (Q neatly / Plotted . . . and / Flatly)
         *Why, was* ed. (Q Why was)
    3   *held in hand* falsely encouraged
         *flatly* completely, utterly
    6   *what ail'st thou* what is wrong with you?
    9   *bravest* finest, most impressive
 9–10  *bottle-nosed* swollen, bottle-shaped
   10  *to* for
        *had.* ed. (Q had)
   11  *rail'st upon* abuse, mock
   12  *bravest* most admirable

ITHAMORE
    Why, know you not?
ABIGAIL
    Why no.                                                                    15
ITHAMORE
    Know you not of Mathias' and Don Lodowick's disaster?
ABIGAIL
    No, what was it?
ITHAMORE
    Why the devil invented a challenge, my master writ it, and
    I carried it, first to Lodowick, and *imprimis* to Mathias.
    And then they met, and as the story says,                                  20
    In doleful wise they ended both their days.
ABIGAIL
    And was my father furtherer of their deaths?
ITHAMORE
    Am I Ithamore?
ABIGAIL
    Yes.
ITHAMORE
    So sure did your father write, and I carry the challenge.                  25
ABIGAIL
    Well, Ithamore, let me request thee this,
    Go to the new-made nunnery, and inquire
    For any of the friars of St Jacques,
    And say, I pray them come and speak with me.
ITHAMORE
    I pray, mistress, will you answer me to one question?                      30
ABIGAIL
    Well, sirrah, what is't?

---

16    *Mathias' . . . Lodowick's* ed. (Q Mathia & Don Lodowick)
19    *imprimis* (Latin) first (Ithamore's error). See his mistaken usage at IV.ii.92.
20    *met, and as* ed. (Q met, as)
21    *In . . . days* Ithamore's deliberately archaic, literary diction, like his obvious delight
      in 'such villainy . . . neatly plotted', his misused Latin and his laughter are reminders
      of his relation to the Vice figure of the earlier stage.
      *doleful wise* sorrowful manner
22    *furtherer* agent
28    *Jacques* ed. (Q Iaynes) Dominican friars, named after their church of St Jacques in
      Paris

ITHAMORE

A very feeling one; have not the nuns fine sport with the friars
now and then?

ABIGAIL

Go to, sirrah sauce, is this your question? Get ye gone.

ITHAMORE

I will forsooth, mistress. *Exit* 35

ABIGAIL

Hard-hearted father, unkind Barabas,
Was this the pursuit of thy policy?
To make me show them favour severally,
That by my favour they should both be slain?
Admit thou lovedst not Lodowick for his sin, 40
Yet Don Mathias ne'er offended thee:
But thou wert set upon extreme revenge,
Because the Prior dispossessed thee once,
And couldst not venge it, but upon his son,
Nor on his son, but by Mathias' means; 45
Nor on Mathias, but by murdering me.
But I perceive there is no love on earth,
Pity in Jews, nor piety in Turks.
But here comes cursed Ithamore with the friar.

*Enter* ITHAMORE, FRIAR [JACOMO]

JACOMO

*Virgo, salve.* 50

ITHAMORE

When, duck you?

---

32–3 ed. (Q A . . . sport / With . . . then?)
32 *a very feeling one* a deeply emotional one (with ironic play on 'feeling' in a physical
sense)
34 *Go to, sirrah sauce* Enough, impudent fellow
*gone* ed. (Q gon)
36 *unkind* unfeeling and/or unnatural
37 *pursuit* direction, outcome
38 *favour* affection
*severally* separately
40 Q's *sinne* is frequently amended to read 'sire', since Lodowick himself has not harmed
Barabas, but the attention of the play to assumptions about morality and inherited
guilt gives Q's wording some claim to interest.
43 *Prior* governing official
50 *Virgo, salve* (Latin) Greetings (God save you), maiden
51 *When, duck you?* ed. (Q When ducke you?) Do you bow? 'When' expresses impatience.

ABIGAIL

  Welcome grave friar: Ithamore be gone.

                              *Exit* [ITHAMORE]

  Know, holy sir, I am bold to solicit thee.

JACOMO

  Wherein?

ABIGAIL

  To get me be admitted for a nun.                          55

JACOMO

  Why Abigail it is not yet long since

  That I did labour thy admission,

  And then thou didst not like that holy life.

ABIGAIL

  Then were my thoughts so frail and unconfirmed,

  And I was chained to follies of the world:                60

  But now experience, purchasèd with grief,

  Has made me see the difference of things.

  My sinful soul, alas, hath paced too long

  The fatal labyrinth of misbelief,

  Far from the Son that gives eternal life.                 65

JACOMO

  Who taught thee this?

ABIGAIL                       The abbess of the house,

  Whose zealous admonition I embrace:

  Oh therefore, Jacomo, let me be one,

  Although unworthy of that sisterhood.

JACOMO

  Abigail I will, but see thou change no more,             70

  For that will be most heavy to thy soul.

ABIGAIL

  That was my father's fault.

JACOMO                        Thy father's, how?

---

55  *To get me be admitted for* To procure my admission as
57  *labour* labour for
59  *unconfirmed* unsettled, unsolidified
65  *Son* ed. (Q *Sonne*) possibly punning on 'sun' and 'son'
67  *admonition* teaching, counsel
68  *Jacomo* ed. (Q *Iacomi*)
71  *heavy* grievous

ABIGAIL

    Nay, you shall pardon me. (Oh Barabas,
    Though thou deservest hardly at my hands,
    Yet never shall these lips bewray thy life.)              75

JACOMO

    Come, shall we go?

ABIGAIL               My duty waits on you.

                                       *Exeunt*

73    *pardon me* excuse me from answering
       ed. (Q Nay, you shall pardon me: oh *Barabas,*)
74    *hardly* severely
75    *bewray* betray

# [ACT III, SCENE iv]

*Enter* BARABAS *reading a letter*

BARABAS

What, Abigail become a nun again?
False, and unkind; what, hast thou lost thy father?
And all unknown, and unconstrained of me,
Art thou again got to the nunnery?
Now here she writes, and wills me to repent.                    5
Repentance? *Spurca*: what pretendeth this?
I fear she knows – 'tis so – of my device
In Don Mathias' and Lodovico's deaths:
If so, 'tis time that it be seen into:
For she that varies from me in belief                           10
Gives great presumption that she loves me not;
Or loving, doth dislike of something done.
But who comes here?

[*Enter* ITHAMORE]

       Oh Ithamore come near;
Come near my love, come near thy master's life,
My trusty servant, nay, my second life;                        15
For I have now no hope but even in thee;
And on that hope my happiness is built:
When saw'st thou Abigail?

ITHAMORE

Today.

BARABAS

With whom?                                                     20

ITHAMORE

A friar.

---

2   *unkind* unnatural (compare III.iii.36)
    *what, hast* ed. (Q what hast)
6   *Spurca* (Italian) filthy
    *pretendeth* signifies
7   ed. (Q I feare she knowes ('tis so) of my deuice)
9   *seen into* looked to
11  *presumption* grounds for presuming
15  *life* Many editions change Q's reading to 'self'.

**BARABAS**

A friar? False villain, he hath done the deed.

**ITHAMORE**

How, sir?

**BARABAS**

Why made mine Abigail a nun.

**ITHAMORE**

That's no lie, for she sent me for him.                                              25

**BARABAS**

O unhappy day,
False, credulous, inconstant Abigail!
But let 'em go: and Ithamore, from hence
Ne'er shall she grieve me more with her disgrace;
Ne'er shall she live to inherit aught of mine,                          30
Be blest of me, nor come within my gates,
But perish underneath my bitter curse
Like Cain by Adam, for his brother's death.

**ITHAMORE**

Oh master.

**BARABAS**

Ithamore, entreat not for her, I am moved,                          35
And she is hateful to my soul and me:
And 'less thou yield to this that I entreat,
I cannot think but that thou hatest my life.

**ITHAMORE**

Who I, master? Why I'll run to some rock and throw myself
headlong into the sea; why I'll do anything for your sweet          40
sake.

**BARABAS**

Oh trusty Ithamore; no servant, but my friend;
I here adopt thee for mine only heir,
All that I have is thine when I am dead,
And whilst I live use half; spend as myself;                          45

---

31   *come within my gates* another of the play's many biblical phrasings (see, e.g.,
Deuteronomy 17.2)

33   *Like Cain by Adam* As elsewhere, Barabas's use of familiar biblical or classical sources
is pointedly ironic or inaccurate. Cain was cursed by God, not by his father Adam,
for killing his brother, and, despite the curse, lived under God's protection (Genesis 4).

35   *moved* emotionally upset

37   *'less* ed. (Q least) unless

39–41   ed. (Q Who . . . and / Throw . . . any / Thing . . . sake.)

Here take my keys, I'll give 'em thee anon:
Go buy thee garments: but thou shalt not want:
Only know this, that thus thou art to do:
But first go fetch me in the pot of rice
That for our supper stands upon the fire.                    50

ITHAMORE

(I hold my head my master's hungry.) I go sir.        *Exit*

BARABAS

Thus every villain ambles after wealth
Although he ne'er be richer than in hope:
But husht.

*Enter* ITHAMORE *with the pot*

ITHAMORE

Here 'tis, master.                                         55

BARABAS

Well said, Ithamore; what, hast thou brought the ladle with
thee too?

ITHAMORE

Yes, sir, the proverb says, he that eats with the devil had need
of a long spoon, I have brought you a ladle.

BARABAS

Very well, Ithamore, then now be secret;                  60
And for thy sake, whom I so dearly love,
Now shalt thou see the death of Abigail,
That thou mayst freely live to be my heir.

ITHAMORE

Why, master, will you poison her with a mess of rice porridge
that will preserve life, make her round and plump, and batten   65
more than you are aware?

---

46–7   Apparently Barabas offers, but does not actually give, Ithamore the keys and wealth
        he promises.
48     *thus thou art to do* this is what you will be able to do
51     (*I . . . hungry.*) *I* ed. (Q I . . . hungry: I)
       *hold* wager
52     *ambles* paces
54     *husht* ed. (Q hush't) be silent
56–7   ed. (Q Well . . . brought / The . . . too?)
56     *what,* ed. (Q what)
58–9   ed. (Q Yes . . . deuil / Had . . . Ladle.)
64     *mess* serving
64–6   ed. (Q Porredge . . . plump, / And . . . aware.)
65     *batten* grow fat          66   *aware?* ed. (Q aware.)

**BARABAS**

Ay but Ithamore seest thou this?
It is a precious powder that I bought
Of an Italian in Ancona once,
Whose operation is to bind, infect,                              70
And poison deeply: yet not appear
In forty hours after it is ta'en.

**ITHAMORE**

How master?

**BARABAS**

Thus Ithamore:
This even they use in Malta here – 'tis called              75
Saint Jacques' Even – and then I say they use
To send their alms unto the nunneries:
Among the rest bear this, and set it there;
There's a dark entry where they take it in,
Where they must neither see the messenger,              80
Nor make enquiry who hath sent it them.

**ITHAMORE**

How so?

**BARABAS**

Belike there is some ceremony in't.
There Ithamore must thou go place this pot:
Stay, let me spice it first.                                          85

**ITHAMORE**

Pray do, and let me help you master. Pray let me taste first.

**BARABAS**

Prithee do: what say'st thou now?

**ITHAMORE**

Troth master, I'm loath such a pot of pottage should be spoiled.

---

69    *Ancona* an Italian port with a history of tolerance towards Jews until their forced
        conversion or expulsion on Papal orders in 1556
70    *bind* constipate
75    *This even they use* This evening they are accustomed to
75–6  *here – 'tis called / Saint Jacques' Even – and* ed. (Q here (tis call'd / Saint *Iagues* Euen)
        and)
83    *Belike* Perhaps
        *ceremony* customary observance
84    *pot* ed.(Q plot)
88    *Troth* In truth, by my faith
        *pottage* soup

**BARABAS**

Peace, Ithamore, 'tis better so than spared.

[BARABAS *puts in poison*]

Assure thyself thou shalt have broth by the eye.                    90

My purse, my coffer, and my self is thine.

**ITHAMORE**

Well, master, I go.

**BARABAS**

Stay, first let me stir it Ithamore.

As fatal be it to her as the draught

Of which great Alexander drunk, and died:                    95

And with her let it work like Borgia's wine,

Whereof his sire, the Pope, was poisonèd.

In few, the blood of Hydra, Lerna's bane;

The juice of hebon, and Cocytus' breath,

And all the poisons of the Stygian pool                    100

Break from the fiery kingdom; and in this

Vomit your venom, and envenom her

That like a fiend hath left her father thus.

*[handwritten margin note: epic poisoning of daughter]*

**ITHAMORE**

What a blessing has he given't! Was ever pot of rice porridge

so sauced? What shall I do with it?                    105

**BARABAS**

Oh my sweet Ithamore go set it down

And come again so soon as thou hast done,

For I have other business for thee.

---

88–9    *spoiled . . . spared* perhaps playing on the biblical notion of sparing the rod and
        spoiling the child (Proverbs 13:24)
   90    *by the eye* abundantly
   95    *great Alexander* One story of Alexander the Great's death (told by Plutarch, among
        others) held that he was poisoned.
   96    *Borgia's wine* Cesare Borgia was reputed to have poisoned his father, Pope Alexander
        VI, in 1503.
   98    *In few* In short
        *Hydra, Lerna's bane* the nine-headed monster slain by Hercules that was troubling
        to Lerna, near Argos, and whose blood was poisonous
   99    *hebon* a poisonous plant, perhaps the yew
        *Cocytus* one of the rivers of Hades
  100    *Stygian* referring to the Styx, the principal river of Hades
 104–5   ed. (Q What . . . of / Rice . . . it?)
  105    *sauced* seasoned

ITHAMORE

Here's a drench to poison a whole stable of Flanders mares:
I'll carry't to the nuns with a powder.                                    110

BARABAS

And the horse pestilence to boot; away.

ITHAMORE

I am gone.
Pay me my wages for my work is done.

*pedring gano*

*Exit*

BARABAS

I'll pay thee with a vengeance Ithamore.

*Exit*

WOW!!
↓
barabas and Ithamore
already have beecf.
he's going to kill
Ithamore!!

109–10    ed. (Q Here's . . . of / Flanders . . . powder.)
   109    *drench* medicinal dose
          *Flanders mares* Belgian horses or lascivious women
   110    *with a powder* quickly and/or with the powdered poison
   111    *horse pestilence* unclear: apparently some horse disease
          *to boot* besides
   114    *with a vengeance* to an extreme degree and/or with a curse

# [ACT III, SCENE v]

*Enter* GOVERNOR [FERNEZE], [MARTIN DEL] BOSCO,
KNIGHTS, BASHAW

FERNEZE
Welcome great Bashaw, how fares Calymath,
What wind drives you thus into Malta road?

BASHAW
The wind that bloweth all the world besides,
Desire of gold.

FERNEZE        Desire of gold, great sir?
That's to be gotten in the Western Ind:      5
In Malta are no golden minerals.

BASHAW
To you of Malta thus saith Calymath:
The time you took for respite is at hand,
For the performance of your promise past;
And for the tribute-money I am sent.      10

FERNEZE
Bashaw, in brief, shalt have no tribute here,
Nor shall the heathens live upon our spoil:
First will we race the city walls ourselves,
Lay waste the island, hew the temples down,
And shipping of our goods to Sicily,      15
Open an entrance for the wasteful sea,
Whose billows beating the resistless banks,
Shall overflow it with their refluence.

BASHAW
Well, Governor, since thou hast broke the league
By flat denial of the promised tribute,      20

---

  1   *Bashaw* ed. (Q *Bashaws*)
  2   As Craik points out, the stress on 'you' here helps to create a sense of Ferneze's
       surprise as feigned; he well knows why the Bashaw has come.
  5   *Western Ind* the Western Hemisphere
  8   *respite is* ed. (Q respite, is)
 12   *spoil* goods, taken in war
 13   *race* raze
 15   *of* Many editors amend to 'off'.
 18   *refluence* flowing back

79

Talk not of racing down your city walls,
You shall not need trouble yourselves so far,
For Selim-Calymath shall come himself,
And with brass bullets batter down your towers,
And turn proud Malta to a wilderness                              25
For these intolerable wrongs of yours;
And so farewell.                                                 [*Exit*]

FERNEZE
Farewell:
And now you men of Malta look about,
And let's provide to welcome Calymath:                            30
Close your portcullis, charge your basilisks,
And as you profitably take up arms,
So now courageously encounter them;
For by this answer, broken is the league,
And nought is to be looked for now but wars,                      35
And nought to us more welcome is than wars.

                                                              *Exeunt*

26–7   ed. (Q *one line*)
  30   *provide* prepare
  31   *portcullis* a grid-like structure which could be lowered to block a gateway
       *basilisks* large cannon
  32   *profitably* beneficially. The sense of more financial sorts of 'profit' is also possible.
  33   *encounter* confront in battle

# [ACT III, SCENE vi]

*Enter two* FRIARS [JACOMO *and* BERNARDINE]

JACOMO
    Oh brother, brother, all the nuns are sick,
    And physic will not help them; they must die.

BERNARDINE
    The abbess sent for me to be confessed:
    Oh what a sad confession will there be!

JACOMO
    And so did fair Maria send for me:            5
    I'll to her lodging; hereabouts she lies.        *Exit*

*Enter* ABIGAIL

BERNARDINE
    What, all dead save only Abigail?

ABIGAIL
    And I shall die too, for I feel death coming.
    Where is the friar that conversed with me?

BERNARDINE
    Oh he is gone to see the other nuns.          10

ABIGAIL
    I sent for him, but seeing you are come
    Be you my ghostly father; and first know,
    That in this house I lived religiously,
    Chaste and devout, much sorrowing for my sins,
    But ere I came –                         15

BERNARDINE
    What then?

ABIGAIL
    I did offend high heaven so grievously,
    As I am almost desperate for my sins:

---

  0.1    ed. (Q *Enter two Fryars and Abigall.*)
  1–3   JACOMO . . . BERNARDINE ed. (Q *1 Fry . . . 2 Fry*)
    2   *physic* medicine
    4   *be!* ed. (Q be?) The question mark in Elizabethan texts often simply registers
        emphasis, not interrogation.
  12   *ghostly father* spiritual confessor
  18   *desperate* despairing of salvation

And one offence torments me more than all.
You knew Mathias and Don Lodowick?                           20

BERNARDINE
Yes, what of them?

ABIGAIL`
⌈ My father did contract me to 'em both:
| First to Don Lodowick, him I never loved;
| Mathias was the man that I held dear,
⌊ And for his sake did I become a nun.                        25

BERNARDINE
So, say how was their end?

ABIGAIL
⌈ Both jealous of my love, envied each other:
| And by my father's practice, which is there
⌊ Set down at large, the gallants were both slain.

                                        [*Gives a paper*]

BERNARDINE
Oh monstrous villainy!                                       30

ABIGAIL
To work my peace, this I confess to thee;
Reveal it not, for then my father dies.

BERNARDINE
Know that confession must not be revealed,
The canon law forbids it, and the priest
That makes it known, being degraded first,                   35
Shall be condemned, and then sent to the fire.

ABIGAIL
So I have heard; pray therefore keep it close,
Death seizeth on my heart, ah gentle friar
Convert my father that he may be saved,
And witness that I die a Christian.           [*Dies*]        40

---

22   *contract* promise, betroth
28   *practice* contrivance, treachery
29   *Set down at large* Written out at length
     *gallants* fine gentlemen, ladies' men
30   *villainy!* ed. (Q villany:)
31   *work my peace* win my absolution
34   *canon law* ecclesiastical law, laid down by the pope and councils
36   *sent to the fire* Bawcutt points out that penalty and possible excommunication might
     follow such violation of canon law, but the death penalty twice mentioned here for
     violating confessional confidentiality is apparently Marlowe's exaggeration.
37   *close* secret

**BERNARDINE**
Ay, and a virgin too, that grieves me most:
But I must to the Jew and exclaim on him,
And make him stand in fear of me.

*Enter* FRIAR [JACOMO]

*creepy...*

*Blackmail*
*Barabas!*

**JACOMO**
Oh brother, all the nuns are dead, let's bury them.

**BERNARDINE**
First help to bury this, then go with me                                    45
And help me to exclaim against the Jew.

**JACOMO**
Why? What has he done?

**BERNARDINE**
A thing that makes me tremble to unfold.

**JACOMO**
What, has he crucified a child?

**BERNARDINE**
No, but a worse thing: 'twas told me in shrift,                           50
Thou know'st 'tis death and if it be revealed.
Come let's away.

*Exeunt [with the body]*

42   *exclaim on* denounce
48   *unfold* explain
49   *What,* ed. (Q What)
      *crucified a child* One traditional legend of anti-Semitism held that Jews crucified
      Christian children.
50   *shrift* confession
51   *and if* if

# ACT IV [SCENE i]

*Enter* BARABAS, ITHAMORE. *Bells within*

BARABAS

    There is no music to a Christian's knell:
    How sweet the bells ring now the nuns are dead
    That sound at other times like tinkers' pans!
    I was afraid the poison had not wrought;
    Or though it wrought, it would have done no good,      5
    For every year they swell, and yet they live;
    Now all are dead, not one remains alive.

ITHAMORE

    That's brave, master, but think you it will not be known?

BARABAS

    How can it if we two be secret?

ITHAMORE

    For my part fear you not.      10

BARABAS

    I'd cut thy throat if I did.

ITHAMORE

    And reason too;
    But here's a royal monastery hard by,
    Good master let me poison all the monks.

BARABAS

    Thou shalt not need, for now the nuns are dead,      15
    They'll die with grief.

ITHAMORE

    Do you not sorrow for your daughter's death?

---

  1   *to* comparable to
      *knell* sound of a bell rung at a funeral
  3   *pans!* ed. (Q pans?)
  4   *wrought* worked
  6   *swell* i.e. from pregnancy
  8   *brave* fine
      *known?* ed. (Q has no end punctuation)
  9   *secret?* ed. (Q secret.)
 12  *And reason too* And with reason too
12–14  ed. (Q And . . . Hard / By . . . Monks.)
 13  *royal* fine, splendid
      *hard by* very near

BARABAS

No, but I grieve because she lived so long
An Hebrew born, and would become a Christian.
*Cazzo, diavola.*                                          20

*Enter the* TWO FRIARS [JACOMO *and* BERNARDINE]

ITHAMORE

Look, look, master, here come two religious caterpillars.

BARABAS

I smelt 'em ere they came.

ITHAMORE

(God-a-mercy nose.) Come let's be gone.

BERNARDINE

Stay wicked Jew, repent, I say, and stay.

JACOMO

Thou hast offended, therefore must be damned.            25

BARABAS

I fear they know we sent the poisoned broth.

ITHAMORE

And so do I, master, therefore speak 'em fair.

BERNARDINE

Barabas, thou hast –

JACOMO

Ay, that thou hast –

BARABAS

True, I have money, what though I have?                   30

BERNARDINE

Thou art a –

JACOMO

Ay, that thou art, a –

BARABAS

What needs all this? I know I am a Jew.

---

18–19   ed. (Q No ... *Hebrew* / Borne ... *diabola.*) Many editors add punctuation after 'long'.
20      *Cazzo, diavola* ed. (Q (marginally) *Catho diabola*); probably an oath derived from
        Italian 'cazzo' for 'penis' and 'diavola' for female devil
21      *caterpillars* parasites upon the social order
23      ed. (Q God-a-mercy nose; come let's begone.)
        *God-a-mercy nose* thanks to your big nose
28–40   For a useful consideration of Barabas's adoption of anti-Semitic discourse, see
        Hodge.

BERNARDINE
Thy daughter –
JACOMO
Ay, thy daughter – 35
BARABAS
Oh speak not of her, then I die with grief.
BERNARDINE
Remember that –
JACOMO
Ay, remember that –
BARABAS
I must needs say that I have been a great usurer.
BERNARDINE
Thou hast committed –
BARABAS                    Fornication? 40
But that was in another country:
And besides, the wench is dead.
BERNARDINE
Ay, but Barabas remember Mathias and Don Lodowick.
BARABAS
Why, what of them?
BERNARDINE
I will not say that by a forged challenge they met. 45
BARABAS
(She has confessed, and we are both undone;)
My bosom inmates (but I must dissemble).
Oh holy friars, the burden of my sins
Lie heavy on my soul; then pray you tell me,
Is't not too late now to turn Christian? 50
I have been zealous in the Jewish faith,
Hard-hearted to the poor, a covetous wretch,
That would for lucre's sake have sold my soul.
A hundred for a hundred I have ta'en;
And now for store of wealth may I compare 55

39    *must needs* have to
40–2  ed. (Q Fornication ... Country: / And ... dead.)
46–7  Q marks 47 '*aside*' and uses italics for 'but I must dissemble' perhaps to signal
      Barabas's progress from conspiratorial aside ('we are both undone') to an address to
      the friars ('My bosom inmates'), to an aside possibly unheard by anyone onstage
      ('*but I must dissemble*').
53    *lucre's* wealth's
54    *A hundred for a hundred* one hundred per cent interest

With all the Jews in Malta; but what is wealth?
I am a Jew, and therefore am I lost.
Would penance serve for this my sin,
I could afford to whip myself to death.

ITHAMORE

And so could I; but penance will not serve.                     60

BARABAS

To fast, to pray, and wear a shirt of hair,
And on my knees creep to Jerusalem.
Cellars of wine, and sollars full of wheat,
Warehouses stuffed with spices and with drugs,
Whole chests of gold, in bullion, and in coin,              65
Besides I know not how much weight in pearl
Orient and round, have I within my house;
At Alexandria, merchandise unsold:
But yesterday two ships went from this town,
Their voyage will be worth ten thousand crowns.          70
In Florence, Venice, Antwerp, London, Seville,
Frankfurt, Lubeck, Moscow, and where not,
Have I debts owing; and in most of these,
Great sums of money lying in the banco;
All this I'll give to some religious house                    75
So I may be baptized and live therein.

JACOMO

Oh good Barabas come to our house.

BERNARDINE

Oh no, good Barabas come to our house.
And Barabas, you know –

BARABAS

I know that I have highly sinned,                            80
You shall convert me, you shall have all my wealth.

---

58    *serve for* serve to atone for
60    Whether or not Ithamore understands Barabas's strategic hypocrisy here, he is
      characteristically uninterested in suffering.
62    *Jerusalem.* ed. (Q *Ierusalem,*)
63    *sollars* lofts
64    *drugs* medicines
65    *bullion* ed. (Q *Bulloine* i.e. Boulogne)
67    *Orient* precious, lustrous
70    *crowns.* ed. (Q crowns)
72    *where not* everywhere
74    *banco* bank

JACOMO

Oh Barabas, their laws are strict.

BARABAS

I know they are, and I will be with you.

BERNARDINE

They wear no shirts, and they go barefoot too.

BARABAS

Then 'tis not for me; and I am resolved                                       85
You shall confess me, and have all my goods.

JACOMO

Good Barabas come to me.

BARABAS

You see I answer him, and yet he stays;
Rid him away, and go you home with me.

BERNARDINE

I'll be with you tonight.                                                      90

BARABAS

Come to my house at one o'clock this night.

JACOMO

You hear your answer, and you may be gone.

BERNARDINE

Why go get you away.

JACOMO

I will not go for thee.

BERNARDINE

Not, then I'll make thee go.                                                   95

JACOMO

How, dost call me rogue?                                    *Fight*

ITHAMORE

Part 'em, master, part 'em.

BARABAS

This is mere frailty, brethren, be content.
Friar Bernardine go you with Ithamore.
You know my mind, let me alone with him.                                       100

---

84–96  The assignment of the friars' speeches has long been a problem; most modern
       editors award line 84 to Bernardine rather than to Q's '1 [Friar]', i.e. Jacomo. On the
       basis of lines 103–5 Craik argues compellingly that Bernardine must have made
       critical remarks about the Dominicans in this passage. In any case the thrust of the
       passage is that each friar naively believes himself in favour with Barabas and, hence,
       in line for his wealth.

   98  *frailty* weakness

100–1  Q gives both lines to Ithamore. Recent editors assume line 100 is intended to

JACOMO

    Why does he go to thy house, let him be gone.

BARABAS

    I'll give him something and so stop his mouth.

           [*Exeunt* ITHAMORE *and* FRIAR BERNARDINE]

    I never heard of any man but he

    Maligned the order of the Jacobins:

    But do you think that I believe his words?           105

    Why brother you converted Abigail;

    And I am bound in charity to requite it,

    And so I will, oh Jacomo, fail not but come.

JACOMO

    But Barabas who shall be your godfathers?

    For presently you shall be shrived.           110

BARABAS

    Marry the Turk shall be one of my godfathers,

    But not a word to any of your covent.

JACOMO

    I warrant thee, Barabas.                *Exit*

BARABAS

    So now the fear is past, and I am safe:

    For he that shrived her is within my house.           115

    What if I murdered him ere Jacomo comes?

    Now I have such a plot for both their lives,

    As never Jew nor Christian knew the like:

    One turned my daughter, therefore he shall die;

    The other knows enough to have my life,           120

    Therefore 'tis not requisite he should live.

    But are not both these wise men to suppose

---

        reassure Bernardine, but Bawcutt points out it is possible that 'let me alone with
        him' could be Ithamore's response to Barabas's own prompting – 'You know my
        mind.'

102    s.d. ed. (Q *Exit*)

104    *Jacobins* Dominicans (see III.iii.28)

109    *godfathers?* ed. (Q godfathers,)

110    *shrived* confessed

111    *the Turk* Ithamore

112    *covent* community, convent

113    *I warrant thee* I give you my promise

115    *house.* ed. (Q house,)

119    *turned* converted

121    *'tis not requisite . . . live* ironic understatement: 'it is not necessary that he live'

That I will leave my house, my goods, and all,
To fast and be well whipped; I'll none of that.
Now Friar Bernardine I come to you,                               125
I'll feast you, lodge you, give you fair words,
And after that, I and my trusty Turk –
No more but so: it must and shall be done.
Ithamore, tell me, is the friar asleep?

*Enter* ITHAMORE

ITHAMORE

Yes; and I know not what the reason is:                          130
Do what I can he will not strip himself,
Nor go to bed, but sleeps in his own clothes;
I fear me he mistrusts what we intend.

BARABAS

No, 'tis an order which the friars use:
Yet if he knew our meanings, could he 'scape?                    135

ITHAMORE

No, none can hear him, cry he ne'er so loud.

BARABAS

Why true, therefore did I place him there:
The other chambers open towards the street.

ITHAMORE

You loiter, master, wherefore stay we thus?
Oh how I long to see him shake his heels.                        140

[*Discovers* FRIAR BERNARDINE *asleep*]

BARABAS

Come on, sirrah,
Off with your girdle, make a handsome noose;
Friar awake.

BERNARDINE

What do you mean to strangle me?

---

  128    *No more but so* Just so, without further ado
  133    *mistrusts* suspects
  134    *order* customary observance
  135    *meanings* intentions
  139    *stay* delay
  140    *shake his heels* i.e. when he is hanged
141–2    ed. (Q *one line*)
  142    *girdle* belt

ITHAMORE

    Yes, 'cause you use to confess.                          145

BARABAS

    Blame not us but the proverb, 'Confess and be hanged'.

    Pull hard.

BERNARDINE

    What, will you have my life?

BARABAS

    Pull hard, I say, you would have had my goods.

ITHAMORE

    Ay, and our lives too, therefore pull amain.             150

    'Tis neatly done, sir, here's no print at all.

BARABAS

    Then is it as it should be, take him up.

ITHAMORE

    Nay, master, be ruled by me a little; so, let him lean upon his

    staff; excellent, he stands as if he were begging of bacon.

BARABAS

    Who would not think but that this friar lived?          155

    What time o' night is't now, sweet Ithamore?

ITHAMORE

    Towards one.

*Enter* [FRIAR] JACOMO

BARABAS

    Then will not Jacomo be long from hence.

                        [*Exeunt* BARABAS *and* ITHAMORE]

JACOMO

    This is the hour wherein I shall proceed;

    Oh happy hour, wherein I shall convert            160

    An infidel, and bring his gold into our treasury.

    But soft, is not this Bernardine? It is;

---

145   *use to confess* make a practice of hearing (and making) confessions; punning on
       religious and judicial meanings

148   *have* ed. (Q saue)

150   *amain* strongly

151   *print* mark on his neck left by the noose

152   *take him up* pick him up and remove him

153   *Nay . . . so* Ithamore stands the friar up as he speaks.

159   *proceed* prosper

162   *But soft* But wait a moment

And understanding I should come this way,
Stands here o' purpose, meaning me some wrong,
And intercept my going to the Jew;                          165
Bernardine!
Wilt thou not speak? Thou think'st I see thee not;
Away, I'd wish thee, and let me go by:
No, wilt thou not? Nay then I'll force my way;
And see, a staff stands ready for the purpose:             170
As thou lik'st that, stop me another time.

*Strike[s] him, he falls.*
*Enter* BARABAS [*and* ITHAMORE]

BARABAS
Why how now Jacomo, what hast thou done?
JACOMO
Why stricken him that would have struck at me.
BARABAS
Who is it, Bernardine? Now out alas, he is slain.
ITHAMORE
Ay, master, he's slain; look how his brains drop out on's nose.   175
JACOMO
Good sirs I have done't, but nobody knows it but you two,
I may escape.
BARABAS
So might my man and I hang with you for company.
ITHAMORE
No, let us bear him to the magistrates.
JACOMO
Good Barabas let me go.                                    180
BARABAS
No, pardon me, the law must have his course.
I must be forced to give in evidence,

---

165  *intercept* to intercept
166–7  ed. (Q And ... *Bernardine*; / Wilt ... not;)
171  *that* i.e. a blow from the staff
174  *it, Bernardine?* ed. (Q it Bernardine?)
     *out alas* exclamation, expressing grief or abhorrence
175  *on's* of his
176–7  ed. (Q Good ... but / You ... escape.)
181  *his* its

That being importuned by this Bernardine
To be a Christian, I shut him out,
And there he sat: now I to keep my word,                    185
And give my goods and substance to your house,
Was up thus early; with intent to go
Unto your friary, because you stayed.

ITHAMORE

Fie upon 'em, master, will you turn Christian, when holy friars
turn devils and murder one another?                    190

BARABAS

No, for this example I'll remain a Jew:
Heaven bless me; what, a friar a murderer?
When shall you see a Jew commit the like?

ITHAMORE

Why a Turk could ha' done no more.

BARABAS

Tomorrow is the sessions; you shall to it.                    195
Come Ithamore, let's help to take him hence.

JACOMO

Villains, I am a sacred person, touch me not.

BARABAS

The law shall touch you, we'll but lead you, we:
'Las I could weep at your calamity.
Take in the staff too, for that must be shown:                    200
Law wills that each particular be known.

                                        *Exeunt.*

183    *importuned* solicited
188    *stayed* delayed coming
189–90    ed. (Q Fie . . . when / Holy . . . another.)
190    *another?* ed. (Q another.)
195    *sessions* when the court sits
199    *'Las* Alas
201    *wills* demands
         *particular* piece of evidence

93

# [ACT IV, SCENE ii]

*call girl* *pimp*

*Enter* COURTESAN [BELLAMIRA] *and* PILIA-BORZA

BELLAMIRA
Pilia-Borza, didst thou meet with Ithamore?

PILIA-BORZA
I did.

BELLAMIRA
And didst thou deliver my letter?

PILIA-BORZA
I did.

BELLAMIRA
And what think'st thou, will he come?                                    5

PILIA-BORZA
I think so, and yet I cannot tell, for at the reading of the letter, he
looked like a man of another world.

BELLAMIRA
Why so?

PILIA-BORZA
That such a base slave as he should be saluted by such a tall man
as I am, from such a beautiful dame as you.                              10

BELLAMIRA
And what said he?

PILIA-BORZA
Not a wise word, only gave me a nod, as who should say, 'Is it
even so?' And so I left him, being driven to a non-plus at the
critical aspect of my terrible countenance.

BELLAMIRA
And where didst meet him?                                               15

---

6–7   ed. (Q I ... of / The ... world.)
  7   *man of another world* spirit
9–10  ed. (Q That ... such / A ... you.)
  9   *saluted* addressed
      *tall* brave, splendid
 10   *dame* fine lady
 12   *as ... say* as if he would say
 13   *even so?' And* ed. (Q euen so; and)
      *non-plus* state of perplexity
 14   *critical aspect* judgemental expression

PILIA-BORZA

Upon mine own freehold within forty foot of the gallows, conning his neck verse I take it, looking of a friar's execution, whom
I saluted with an old hempen proverb, *Hodie tibi, cras mihi,* and
so I left him to the mercy of the hangman: but the exercise being
done, see where he comes.                                                    20

*Enter* ITHAMORE

ITHAMORE

I never knew a man take his death so patiently as this friar; he
was ready to leap off ere the halter was about his neck; and when
the hangman had put on his hempen tippet, he made such haste
to his prayers, as if he had had another cure to serve; well, go
whither he will, I'll be none of his followers in haste: and now     25
I think on't, going to the execution, a fellow met me with a
muschatoes like a raven's wing, and a dagger with a hilt like a
warming-pan, and he gave me a letter from one Madam Bellamira, saluting me in such sort as if he had meant to make clean
my boots with his lips; the effect was, that I should come to her     30
house, I wonder what the reason is; it may be she sees more in
me than I can find in myself: for she writes further, that she
loves me ever since she saw me, and who would not requite such
love? Here's her house, and here she comes, and now would
I were gone, I am not worthy to look upon her.                             35

16–20    ed. (Q Vpon . . . the / Gallowes . . . a / Fryars . . . hempen / prouerb . . . mercy / Of . . .
         where / He comes.)
16       *freehold* literally, land held as private estate; here perhaps the location of Pilia-Borza's
         career as pickpocket
16–17    *conning* studying
17       *neck verse* the Latin verse (generally Psalm 51) that the criminal must be able to read
         in order to claim 'benefit of clergy' and thereby escape punishment
         *looking of* looking at
18       *hempen* referring to the hangman's rope
         *Hodie . . . mihi* ed. (Q *Hidie . . . mihi*); (Latin) today you; tomorrow me
19–20    *exercise being done* religious service being over
21–35    ed. (Q I . . . as / This . . . was / About . . . his / Hempen . . . if / Hee . . . wh ther / He . . .
         haste: / And . . . fellow / Met . . . and / A . . . he / Gaue . . . *Belamira,* / Saluting . . . make /
         Cleane . . . that / I . . . is; / It . . . in / My . . . me / Euer . . . such / Loue . . . now / Would . . .
         her.)
23       *tippet* the scarf worn around a priest's neck
24       *cure to serve* parish to minister to
27       *muschatoes* moustache
28       *warming-pan* long-handled pan used for warming beds
30       *effect* upshot

PILIA-BORZA

This is the gentleman you writ to.

ITHAMORE

('Gentleman', he flouts me, what gentry can be in a poor Turk
of ten pence? I'll be gone.)

BELLAMIRA

Is't not a sweet-faced youth, Pilia?

ITHAMORE

(Again, 'sweet youth'.) Did not you, sir, bring the sweet youth    40
a letter?

PILIA-BORZA

I did sir, and from this gentlewoman, who as myself, and the
rest of the family, stand or fall at your service.

BELLAMIRA

Though woman's modesty should hale me back, I can withhold
no longer; welcome sweet love.                                     45

ITHAMORE

(Now am I clean, or rather foully out of the way.)

BELLAMIRA

Whither so soon?

ITHAMORE

(I'll go steal some money from my master to make me handsome.) Pray pardon me, I must go see a ship discharged.

BELLAMIRA

Canst thou be so unkind to leave me thus?                          50

PILIA-BORZA

And ye did but know how she loves you, sir.

---

37–8    ed. (Q Gentleman . . . a / Poore . . . gone.)
  37    *flouts* mocks
37–8    *Turk of ten pence* i.e. worthless person
40–1    ed. (Q Agen sweet youth; did not you, Sir, bring the sweet / Youth a letter?)
42–3    ed. (Q I . . . my / Selfe . . . seruice.)
  43    *family* household
        *fall* with sexual connotation
  44    *hale* pull
  46    *clean* completely (with a pun contrasting 'foully')
        *out of the way* out of my depth; bewildered
48–9    ed. (Q I'le . . . to / Make . . . hansome: / Pray . . . discharg'd.)
  49    *discharged* unloaded
  51    *And* If

ITHAMORE

Nay, I care not how much she loves me; sweet Allamira, would I
had my master's wealth for thy sake.

PILIA-BORZA

And you can have it, sir, and if you please.

ITHAMORE

If 'twere above ground I could, and would have it; but he hides     55
and buries it up as partridges do their eggs, under the earth.

PILIA-BORZA

And is't not possible to find it out?

ITHAMORE

By no means possible.

BELLAMIRA

(What shall we do with this base villain then?

PILIA-BORZA

Let me alone, do but you speak him fair.)     60
But you know some secrets of the Jew, which if they were revealed,
would do him harm.

*[handwritten margin note: people know Ithamore knows stuff about barabas and loose end]*

ITHAMORE

Ay, and such as – Go to, no more, I'll make him send me half he
has, and glad he scapes so too. Pen and ink: I'll write unto him,
we'll have money straight.     65

PILIA-BORZA

Send for a hundred crowns at least.

ITHAMORE

Ten hundred thousand crowns, – (*He writes*) 'Master Barabas'.

PILIA-BORZA

Write not so submissively, but threatening him.

---

52–3    ed. (Q Nay . . . me; / Sweet . . . sake.)
52      *Allamira* Although Q frequently employs variant forms of characters' names, this
        variation suggests misspeaking.
54      *and if* if
55–6    ed. (Q If . . . it; / But . . . doe / Their . . . earth.)
60      ed. (Q Let . . . fair:)
        *Let me alone* Leave it to me
        *speak him fair* talk sweetly to him
63–5    ed. (Q I . . . more / I'le . . . too. / Pen and Inke: / I'le . . . strait.)
63      *Go to* (exclamation) Go on; Come, come
64      *scapes* escapes
65      *straight* right away
67      *He writes* (marginally after line 66 in Q)

ITHAMORE

'Sirrah Barabas, send me a hundred crowns.'

PILIA-BORZA

Put in two hundred at least.                                                           70

ITHAMORE

'I charge thee send me three hundred by this bearer, and this
    shall be your warrant; if you do not, no more but so.'

PILIA-BORZA

Tell him you will confess.

ITHAMORE

'Otherwise I'll confess all.' Vanish and return in a twinkle.

PILIA-BORZA

Let me alone, I'll use him in his kind.                        [*Exit*]    75

ITHAMORE

Hang him Jew.

BELLAMIRA

Now, gentle Ithamore, lie in my lap.
    Where are my maids? Provide a running banquet;
    Send to the merchant, bid him bring me silks,
    Shall Ithamore my love go in such rags?                                   80

ITHAMORE

And bid the jeweller come hither too.

BELLAMIRA

I have no husband, sweet, I'll marry thee.

ITHAMORE

Content, but we will leave this paltry land,
    And sail from hence to Greece, to lovely Greece,
    I'll be thy Jason, thou my golden fleece;                                  85

  69    *Sirrah* a disrespectful form of address (see I.i.70)
71–2    ed. (Q I ... this / Shall ... so.)
  72    *no more but so* As Craik points out, this vague threat – something like 'you know
          what I mean' – is given a more precise form by Pilia-Borza's subsequent suggestions.
  74    *all.' Vanish* ed. (Q all, vanish)
          *in a twinkle* instantly
  75    *use* treat
          *in his kind* according to his nature. Bawcutt (citing Tilley, J 52) observes that to 'use
          someone like a Jew' later became proverbial for ill-treatment.
  77    *lie in my lap* used with sexual implication
  78    *running banquet* hastily prepared banquet
  83    *Content* Agreed
  85    *Jason ... fleece* According to the Greek myth, Jason and the Argonauts recovered the
          magical golden fleece from Colchis.

Where painted carpets o'er the meads are hurled, —*romantic*
And Bacchus' vineyards o'er-spread the world:
Where woods and forests go in goodly green,
I'll be Adonis, thou shalt be Love's Queen.
The meads, the orchards, and the primrose lanes,          90
Instead of sedge and reed, bear sugar canes:
Thou in those groves, by Dis above,
Shalt live with me and be my love.

BELLAMIRA
Whither will I not go with gentle Ithamore?

*Enter* PILIA-BORZA

ITHAMORE
How now? Hast thou the gold?                              95

PILIA-BORZA
Yes.

ITHAMORE
But came it freely, did the cow give down her milk freely?

PILIA-BORZA
At reading of the letter, he stared and stamped and turned
aside, I took him by the beard, and looked upon him thus; told
him he were best to send it, then he hugged and embraced me.   100

ITHAMORE
Rather for fear than love.

PILIA-BORZA
Then like a Jew he laughed and jeered, and told me he loved me
for your sake, and said what a faithful servant you had been.

---

86    *painted carpets* used metaphorically for bright flowers
      *meads* meadows
87    *Bacchus* Roman name for Dionysus, god of wine
88    *go* are dressed in
89    *Adonis . . . Love's Queen* In classical myth and verse, Adonis was a beautiful youth
      beloved by Venus, goddess of love.
91    *sedge* coarse grass
92    *Dis* Roman god (Greek Hades, Pluto) of the underworld; i.e. by no means 'above'
93    This alludes (probably parodically) to Marlowe's own lyric 'The Passionate Shepherd
      to his Love', which begins 'Come live with me and be my love'. — *LoL*
97    *give down her milk* let flow her milk
98–100  ed. (Q At . . . turnd / Aside . . . thus; / Told . . . me.)
98    *stared* ed. (Q sterd)
99    *took him by the beard* a serious insult
      *thus* an indication of staged action (see I.ii.347)

ITHAMORE

The more villain he to keep me thus: here's goodly 'parel, is there
not?                                                                      105

PILIA-BORZA

To conclude, he gave me ten crowns.

ITHAMORE

But ten? I'll not leave him worth a grey groat, give me a ream
of paper, we'll have a kingdom of gold for't.

PILIA-BORZA

Write for five hundred crowns.

ITHAMORE

[*Writes*] 'Sirrah Jew, as you love your life send me five hundred     110
crowns, and give the bearer one hundred.' Tell him I must have't.

PILIA-BORZA

I warrant your worship shall have't.

ITHAMORE

And if he ask why I demand so much, tell him,
I scorn to write a line under a hundred crowns.

PILIA-BORZA

You'd make a rich poet, sir. I am gone.                        *Exit*   115

ITHAMORE

Take thou the money, spend it for my sake.

BELLAMIRA

'Tis not thy money, but thy self I weigh:
Thus Bellamira esteems of gold;                    [*Throws it aside*]
But thus of thee.                                   *Kiss*[*es*] *him*

ITHAMORE

That kiss again; she runs division of my lips.                         120
What an eye she casts on me! It twinkles like a star.

BELLAMIRA

Come my dear love, let's in and sleep together.

---

104–5   ed. (Q The ... thus: / Here's ... not?)
104    '*parel* clothing
106    *ten crowns* as a tip
107–8   ed. (Q But. .. giue / Me ... for't.)
107    *grey groat* i.e. an insignificant amount
       *ream* a large amount of paper (480 sheets or more); with an apparent pun on 'realm'
110–11  ed. (Q Sirra ... crowns, / And ... hau't.)
111    *one hundred* ed. (Q 100)
117    *weigh* value
120    *runs division of* plays musically upon
121    *me!* ed. (Q What ... me? / It ... Starre.)

ITHAMORE

Oh that ten thousand nights were put in one,

that we might sleep seven years together afore we wake.

BELLAMIRA

Come amorous wag, first banquet and then sleep.                125

[*Exeunt*]

---

123–4    Cra k accurately sums up this speech as 'Marlowesque verse, tailing off into bathetic
              prose'.
   124    ed. (Q That . . . afore / We wake.)
   125    *wag* a term of endearment, impudent youth

# [ACT IV, SCENE iii]

*Enter* BARABAS *reading a letter*

BARABAS
    'Barabas send me three hundred crowns.'
    Plain Barabas: Oh that wicked courtesan!
    He was not wont to call me Barabas.
    'Or else I will confess': ay, there it goes:
    But if I get him *coupe de gorge*, for that.          5
    He sent a shaggy tottered staring slave,
    That when he speaks, draws out his grisly beard,
    And winds it twice or thrice about his ear;
    Whose face has been a grindstone for men's swords,
    His hands are hacked, some fingers cut quite off;      10
    Who when he speaks, grunts like a hog, and looks
    Like one that is employed in catzerie,
    And crossbiting, such a rogue
    As is the husband to a hundred whores:
    And I by him must send three hundred crowns.      15
    Well, my hope is, he will not stay there still;
    And when he comes: Oh that he were but here!

*Enter* PILIA-BORZA

PILIA-BORZA
    Jew, I must ha' more gold.

---

3    *wont* accustomed
4    *there it goes* i.e. this shows his intentions
5    *coupe de gorge* (French) [I'll] cut [his] throat
      *that.* ed. (Q that)
6    *tottered* tattered
      *staring* looking fixedly, with wide-open eyes
7    *grisly* grim, ghastly
12    *in catzerie* i.e. in pimping; from Italian 'cazzo' (compare IV.i.20)
13    *crossbiting,* ed. (Q crossbiting)
      *crossbiting* cheating (probably implying reciprocity, as in wronging a wrongdoer)
14    *husband . . . whores* i.e. either a pimp who 'husbands' the resources of a hundred
      prostitutes, or a swindler who claims to be the husband of prostitutes in order to
      blackmail their clients
16    *still* forever

**BARABAS**

Why want'st thou any of thy tale?

**PILIA-BORZA**

No; but three hundred will not serve his turn.                      20

**BARABAS**

Not serve his turn, sir?

**PILIA-BORZA**

No sir; and therefore I must have five hundred more.

**BARABAS**

I'll rather –

**PILIA-BORZA**

Oh good words, sir, and send it you were best; see, there's his
letter.                                                             25

**BARABAS**

Might he not as well come as send? Pray bid him come and
fetch it; what he writes for you, ye shall have straight.

**PILIA-BORZA**

Ay, and the rest too, or else –

**BARABAS**

(I must make this villain away.) Please you dine with me, sir,
and you shall be most heartily (poisoned).                         30

**PILIA-BORZA**

No god-a-mercy, shall I have these crowns?

**BARABAS**

I cannot do it, I have lost my keys.

**PILIA-BORZA**

Oh, if that be all, I can pick ope your locks.

**BARABAS**

Or climb up to my counting-house window: you know my
meaning.                                                           35

---

19    *want'st . . . tale?* are you missing any of your desired amount?
20    *serve his turn* be sufficient for his purposes
24–5  ed. (Q Oh . . . see, / There's . . . letter.)
24    *good words* do not speak so aggressively (compare V.ii.61)
26–7  ed. (Q Might . . . him / Come . . . streight.)
27    *what . . . for you* the bearer's hundred crowns (compare IV.ii.111)
29    ed. (Q away: please)
29–30  ed. (Q I . . . dine / With . . . poyson'd.) Q's marginal '*aside*' does not indicate how
       much of this speech is aside; compare Barabas's unexpected final words (e.g.
       II.iii.67).
34–5  ed. (Q Or . . . window: / You . . . meaning.) Barabas implies knowledge of the
       burglary attempt in III.i.

PILIA-BORZA

I know enough, and therefore talk not to me of your counting-
house; the gold, or know Jew it is in my power to hang thee.

BARABAS

(I am betrayed.)
'Tis not five hundred crowns that I esteem,
I am not moved at that: this angers me,           40
That he who knows I love him as myself
Should write in this imperious vein! Why sir,
You know I have no child, and unto whom
Should I leave all but unto Ithamore?

PILIA-BORZA

Here's many words but no crowns; the crowns.        45

BARABAS

Commend me to him, sir, most humbly,
And unto your good mistress as unknown.

PILIA-BORZA

Speak, shall I have 'em, sir?

BARABAS

Sir here they are.               *[Gives gold]*
(Oh that I should part with so much gold!)      50
Here take 'em, fellow, with as good a will –
(As I would see thee hanged.) Oh, love stops my breath:
Never loved man servant as I do Ithamore.

PILIA-BORZA

I know it, sir.

BARABAS

Pray when, sir, shall I see you at my house?      55

PILIA-BORZA

Soon enough to your cost, sir: fare you well.      *Exit*

BARABAS

Nay to thine own cost, villain, if thou com'st.
Was ever Jew tormented as I am?
To have a shag-rag knave to come –

---

36–7   *counting-house;* ed. (Q Counting-house,)
  42   *vein!* ed. (Q vaine?)     *vein* manner, style
  47   *as unknown* a polite locution: unknown to Barabas
  52   ed. (Q – *As I wud see thee hang'd* oh, loue stops my breath:)
  56   ed. (Q Soone . . . Sir: / Fare . . . well.)
  59   *shag-rag* ragged
       *come –* ed. (Q come) Many editors conjecture a missing word such as 'demand' or
       'convey' after 'come'.

ACT IV SCENE iii

Three hundred crowns, and then five hundred crowns?          60
Well, I must seek a means to rid 'em all,
And presently: for in his villainy
He will tell all he knows and I shall die for't.
I have it.
I will in some disguise go see the slave,                    65
And how the villain revels with my gold.              *Exit*

---

61   *rid* remove by violence, kill
62   *presently* immediately
63–4   ed. (Q *one line*)

105

# [ACT IV, SCENE iv]

*Enter* COURTESAN [BELLAMIRA], ITHAMORE, PILIA-BORZA

BELLAMIRA
I'll pledge thee, love, and therefore drink it off.

ITHAMORE
Say'st thou me so? Have at it; and do you hear?

[*Whispers to her*]

BELLAMIRA
Go to, it shall be so.

ITHAMORE
Of that condition, I will drink it up; here's to thee.

BELLAMIRA
Nay, I'll have all or none.                                                    5

ITHAMORE
There, if thou lov'st me do not leave a drop.

BELLAMIRA
Love thee, fill me three glasses.

ITHAMORE
Three and fifty dozen, I'll pledge thee.

PILIA-BORZA
Knavely spoke, and like a knight at arms.

ITHAMORE
Hey *Rivo Castiliano*, a man's a man.                                     10

2    *me* to me
4    *Of* On
5    BELLAMIRA ed. (Q Pil.) As Bawcutt argues, attribution of this line to Bellamira
     makes sense, both because she is engaged in a ritual of drinking toasts with Ithamore
     and because she has reasons to encourage him to get drunk.
8    *thee.* ed. (Q thee,)
9    *Knavely spoke.* Craik's argument that this phrase plays on 'bravely spoke' (as in
     'bravely done' in line 18) with a clever antithesis between 'knave' and 'knight' is
     attractive, since this figure would compactly render Pilia-Borza's contempt for
     Ithamore and his drunken version of romantic exuberance.
10   *Rivo Castiliano* 'Rivo' is perhaps derived from Spanish *arriba* (up, upwards) and
     appears by itself as a drinker's cry (compare *I Henry IV* II.iv.108–9). 'Rivo Castiliano'
     could also be Italian for 'River of Castile', and thus might suggest a wish for Spanish
     wine.
     *a man's a man* a proverbial assertion of human equality despite social distinction
     (compare Tilley, M 243 and Iago's drinking song with 'A soldier's a man' in *Othello*
     II.iii.66)

BELLAMIRA

Now to the Jew.

ITHAMORE

Ha to the Jew, and send me money you were best.

PILIA-BORZA

What would'st thou do if he should send thee none?

ITHAMORE

Do nothing; but I know what I know, he's a murderer.

BELLAMIRA

I had not thought he had been so brave a man. 15

ITHAMORE

You knew Mathias and the Governor's son, he and I killed 'em
both, and yet never touched 'em.

PILIA-BORZA

Oh bravely done.

ITHAMORE

I carried the broth that poisoned the nuns, and he and I,
snickle hand too fast, strangled a friar. 20

BELLAMIRA

You two alone.

ITHAMORE

We two, and 'twas never known, nor never shall be for me.

PILIA-BORZA

(This shall with me unto the Governor.

BELLAMIRA

And fit it should: but first let's ha' more gold!)
Come gentle Ithamore, lie in my lap. 25

---

12  *Ha to the Jew* Craik argues that Ithamore responds to the offer of an ironic toast to
    Barabas in the previous line; but it appears more likely that Bellamira proposes
    Ithamore turn his attention to extorting money from Barabas and that he here
    begins dictating his letter to that effect.
    *you* i.e. Barabas

14  ed. (Q Doe . . . know / He's a murderer.)

16–17  ed. (Q You . . . and / I . . . 'em.)

19–20  ed. (Q I . . . he / And . . . Fryar.)
    *I, snickle hand too fast,* ed. (Q I snicle hand too fast,) Unclear; 'snickle' may mean
    'snare', so the phrase could mean 'I, with my snaring hand too fast to be escaped'.
    'Hand to fist' – a stock phrase for hand to hand combat – has been suggested; while
    Craik follows Kittredge in punctuating as reiterated dialogue 'snicle! hand to! fast!'

22  ed. (Q We . . . shall / Be for me.)
    *for me* so far as I am concerned

25  *lie* suggesting sexual intercourse

little, love me long, let music rumble,
n thy incony lap do tumble.

*Enter* BARABAS *with a lute, disguised*

**BELLAMIRA**
A French musician, come let's hear your skill?
**BARABAS**
Must tuna my lute for sound, twang twang first.
**ITHAMORE**
Wilt drink Frenchman, here's to thee with a – Pox on this       30
drunken hiccup.
**BARABAS**
Gramercy monsieur.
**BELLAMIRA**
Prithee, Pilia-Borza, bid the fiddler give me the posy in his hat
there.
**PILIA-BORZA**
Sirrah, you must give my mistress your posy.       35
**BARABAS**
*A vôtre commandement madame.*
**BELLAMIRA**
How sweet, my Ithamore, the flowers smell.
**ITHAMORE**
Like thy breath, sweetheart, no violet like 'em.
**PILIA-BORZA**
Foh, methinks they stink like a hollyhock.
**BARABAS**
(So, now I am revenged upon 'em all.       40
The scent thereof was death, I poisoned it.)

---

26    *Love me little, love me long* proverbial (Tilley, L 559)
27    *incony* ed. (Q incoomy) attractive, with an obscene pun, as Craik notes, on 'coney'
       as used in Marlowe's translation of Ovid's *Elegies* (I.x): 'The whore stands to be
       bought for each man's money, / And seeks vile wealth by selling of her coney'.
30    ed. (Q Wilt . . . a – / Pox . . . hick-vp.)
       *Pox* an oath; literally, venereal disease
32    *Gramercy* Thank you
33–4  ed. (Q Prethe . . . me / The . . . there.)
       *posy* bouquet
36    *A vôtre commandement* (French) At your command

**ITHAMORE**
  Play, fiddler, or I'll cut your cats' guts into chitterlings.
**BARABAS**
  *Pardonnez-moi*, be no in tune yet; so now, now all be in.
**ITHAMORE**
  Give him a crown, and fill me out more wine.
**PILIA-BORZA**
  There's two crowns for thee, play.                           45
**BARABAS**
  (How liberally the villain gives me mine own gold.)
**PILIA-BORZA**
  Methinks he fingers very well.
**BARABAS**
  (So did you when you stole my gold.)
**PILIA-BORZA**
  How swift he runs.
**BARABAS**
  (You run swifter when you threw my gold out of my window.)   50
**BELLAMIRA**
  Musician, hast been in Malta long?
**BARABAS**
  Two, three, four month madame.
**ITHAMORE**
  Dost not know a Jew, one Barabas?
**BARABAS**
  Very mush, monsieur, you no be his man.
**PILIA-BORZA**
  His man?                                                     55
**ITHAMORE**
  I scorn the peasant, tell him so.
**BARABAS**
  (He knows it already.)

42  *cats' guts . . . chitterlings* lute strings . . . pork sausages
43  *Pardonnez-moi* ed. (Q Pardona moy) (French) Pardon me. It is not clear whether
    Barabas's French is intended to be as corrupt as his accented English in this scene.
44  *fill me out* pour for me
46  Q has a marginal '*aside*' here and at lines 48, 50, 60, 62 and 65.
47  *fingers* plays (with a pun on 'pilfering' that is picked up in Barabas's next line)
49  *runs* executes a rapid sequence of notes
50  ed. (Q You . . . of / My Window.)
54  *man* servant (this line is often made a question)

ITHAMORE

'Tis a strange thing of that Jew, he lives upon pickled grass-
hoppers, and sauced mushrumbs.

BARABAS

(What a slave's this? The Governor feeds not as I do.) 60

ITHAMORE

He never put on clean shirt since he was circumcised.

BARABAS

(Oh rascal! I change myself twice a day.)

ITHAMORE

The hat he wears, Judas left under the elder when he hanged
himself.

BARABAS

('Twas sent me for a present from the great Cham.) 65

PILIA-BORZA

A masty slave he is; whither now, fiddler?

BARABAS

*Pardonnez moi, monsieur,* we be no well. *Exit*

PILIA-BORZA

Farewell fiddler: one letter more to the Jew.

BELLAMIRA

Prithee sweet love, one more, and write it sharp.

ITHAMORE

No, I'll send by word of mouth now; bid him deliver thee a 70
thousand crowns, by the same token, that the nuns loved rice,
that Friar Bernardine slept in his own clothes, any of 'em
will do it.

---

58–9 ed. (Q 'Tis ... vpon / Pickled ... Mushrumbs.)
59 *sauced mushrumbs* seasoned mushrooms
60 ed. (Q What ... this? / The ... doe.)
61 *circumcised.* ed. (Q circumcis'd)
63–4 ed. (Q The ... Elder / When ... himselfe.)
    *Judas ... himself* See Matthew 27; the elder tree is traditional, but the hat is
apparently Marlowe's invention.
65 *great Cham* emperor (Khan) of the Mongols, Tartars and Chinese
66 ed. (Q A ... is; / Whether ... Fidler?)
    *masty* fattened, as a swine; or big-bodied. Craik amends to 'nasty', and Bawcutt sug-
gests 'musty', but the metaphor of swinishness and the repulsive sense of physicality
are appropriate to the prejudices of the speakers.
    *whither* ed. (Q whether)
69 *sharp* sharply worded
70–3 ed. (Q No ... now; / Bid ... same / Token ... *Bernardine* / Slept ... clothes, / Any ... it.)

PILIA-BORZA

　　Let me alone to urge it now I know the meaning.

ITHAMORE

　　The meaning has a meaning; come let's in:　　　　　　　　75
　　To undo a Jew is charity, and not sin.

　　　　　　　　　　　　　　　　　　　　　*Exeunt*

---

75　　*The meaning has a meaning* Unclear; perhaps Ithamore pretends sagacity and deep
　　　policy – such pretension would maintain his general parallelism with Barabas.

# ACT V [SCENE i]

*Enter* GOVERNOR [FERNEZE], KNIGHTS, MARTIN DEL BOSCO
[*and* OFFICERS]

FERNEZE

Now, gentlemen, betake you to your arms,
And see that Malta be well fortified;
And it behoves you to be resolute;
For Calymath having hovered here so long,
Will win the town, or die before the walls.                    5

KNIGHT

And die he shall, for we will never yield.

*Enter* COURTESAN [BELLAMIRA] *and* PILIA-BORZA

BELLAMIRA

Oh bring us to the Governor.

FERNEZE

Away with her, she is a courtesan.

BELLAMIRA

Whate'er I am, yet Governor hear me speak;
I bring thee news by whom thy son was slain:        10
Mathias did it not, it was the Jew.

PILIA-BORZA

Who, besides the slaughter of these gentlemen,
Poisoned his own daughter and the nuns,
Strangled a friar, and I know not what
Mischief beside.

FERNEZE                    Had we but proof of this.          15

BELLAMIRA

Strong proof, my lord, his man's now at my lodging
That was his agent, he'll confess it all.

FERNEZE

Go fetch him straight,

[*Exeunt* OFFICERS]
I always feared that Jew.

---

6   *KNIGHT* Many editors designate as 1 Knight.
16–17   ed. (Q Strong . . . my / Lodging . . . all.)
18   *straight* immediately

112

*Enter* [OFFICERS *with*] JEW [BARABAS], ITHAMORE

BARABAS

I'll go alone, dogs do not hale me thus.

ITHAMORE

Nor me neither, I cannot outrun you constable, oh my belly.            20

BARABAS

(One dram of powder more had made all sure,
What a damned slave was I!)

FERNEZE

Make fires, heat irons, let the rack be fetched.

KNIGHT

Nay stay, my lord, 't may be he will confess.

BARABAS

Confess; what mean you, lords, who should confess?            25

FERNEZE

Thou and thy Turk; 'twas you that slew my son.

ITHAMORE

Guilty, my lord, I confess; your son and Mathias
Were both contracted unto Abigail,
Forged a counterfeit challenge.

BARABAS

Who carried that challenge?            30

ITHAMORE

I carried it, I confess, but who writ it? Marry even he that
strangled Bernardine, poisoned the nuns, and his own daughter.

FERNEZE

Away with him, his sight is death to me.

BARABAS

For what? You men of Malta, hear me speak;
She is a courtesan and he a thief,            35
And he my bondman, let me have law,

19    *hale* drag
20    To 'outrun the constable' is proverbial (Tilley, C 615).
22    *damned slave* fool
      *I!* ed. (Q I?)
29    Many editors insert an initial 'he', although in the light of questions about agency in
      this scene, it may be worthwhile to keep the ambiguity of Ithamore's phrasing.
31–2  ed. (Q I . . . it? / Marry . . . the / Nuns . . . daughter.)
31    *Marry* interjection, 'Why, to be sure'
33    Compare in *The Spanish Tragedy* the Viceroy's irate dismissal of the man he believes
      to have murdered his son – 'Away with him, his sight is second hell' (I.iii.89).
36    *bondman* slave, serf

For none of this can prejudice my life.

FERNEZE

Once more away with him; you shall have law.

BARABAS

Devils do your worst, I live in spite of you.

As these have spoke so be it to their souls. 40

(I hope the poisoned flowers will work anon.) *foster*

> [*Exeunt* OFFICERS *with* BARABAS, ITHAMORE,
> BELLAMIRA, *and* PILIA-BORZA]

*Enter* [MATHIAS'S] MOTHER [KATHERINE]

KATHERINE

Was my Mathias murdered by the Jew?

Ferneze, 'twas thy son that murdered him.

FERNEZE

Be patient, gentle madam, it was he,

He forged the daring challenge made them fight. 45

KATHERINE

Where is the Jew, where is that murderer?

FERNEZE

In prison till the law has passed on him.

*Enter* OFFICER

OFFICER

My lord, the courtesan and her man are dead;

So is the Turk, and Barabas the Jew.

FERNEZE

Dead? 50

---

36–40   *let me have law . . . you shall have law* Echoes of this phrasing in Shakespeare's
*Merchant of Venice* are pronounced: Shylock's demand 'I crave the law' (IV.i.204)
and Portia's ironic acquiescence 'The Jew shall have all justice' (319) accentuate the
play's representation of values and communities in confrontation. The charge of
legalism has been a traditional feature of Christian responses to Judaism.

37   *life.* ed. (Q life:)

39   *Devils . . . you* These lines are frequently considered to be an aside, and many editors
amend Q's 'I live' to 'I'll live', but the defiance in Barabas's voice is elsewhere evident
in this scene, and 'I live in spite of you' is a notable instance of that heroic discourse
which frequently comes in for ironic treatment in the play (e.g. II.ii.56).

40–1   ed. (Q As . . . soules: / I . . . anon.)

40   *so be it to* so let it be charged against

41   *anon* immediately

47   *passed* passed judgement

OFFICER

Dead, my lord, and here they bring his body.

[*Enter* OFFICERS, *carrying* BARABAS *as dead*]

BOSCO

This sudden death of his is very strange.

FERNEZE

Wonder not at it, sir, the heavens are just.

Their deaths were like their lives, then think not of 'em.

Since they are dead, let them be buried. 55

For the Jew's body, throw that o'er the walls,

To be a prey for vultures and wild beasts.

[BARABAS *thrown down*]

So, now away and fortify the town.

*Exeunt* [*all except* BARABAS]

BARABAS

What, all alone? Well fare sleepy drink.

I'll be revenged on this accursèd town; 60

For by my means Calymath shall enter in.

I'll help to slay their children and their wives,

To fire the churches, pull their houses down,

Take my goods too, and seize upon my lands:

I hope to see the Governor a slave, 65

And, rowing in a galley, whipped to death.

*Enter* CALYMATH, BASHAWS, TURKS

CALYMATH

Whom have we there, a spy?

BARABAS

Yes, my good lord, one that can spy a place

Where you may enter, and surprise the town:

My name is Barabas; I am a Jew. 70

CALYMATH

Art thou that Jew whose goods we heard were sold

For tribute money?

58  *So* A typical indication of the accomplishment of stage action; presumably Barabas's body is here thrown 'o'er the walls'. Subsequent lines are delivered from outside the city walls.

59  *Well fare* Blessings on
   *sleepy* sleep-inducing

62–3  This is a typically Marlovian invocation of destruction (see *Edward II* I.iv.100–2; *Massacre at Paris* V.v.61–4).

**BARABAS**        The very same, my lord:
And since that time they have hired a slave my man
To accuse me of a thousand villainies:
I was imprisoned, but 'scaped their hands.      75

**CALYMATH**
Didst break prison?

**BARABAS**
No, no:
I drank of poppy and cold mandrake juice;
And being asleep, belike they thought me dead,
And threw me o'er the walls: so, or how else,      80
The Jew is here, and rests at your command.

**CALYMATH**
'Twas bravely done: but tell me, Barabas,
Canst thou, as thou reportest, make Malta ours?

**BARABAS**
Fear not, my lord, for here against the sluice,
The rock is hollow, and of purpose digged,      85
To make a passage for the running streams
And common channels of the city.
Now whilst you give assault unto the walls,
I'll lead five hundred soldiers through the vault,
And rise with them i' th' middle of the town,      90
Open the gates for you to enter in,
And by this means the city is your own.

**CALYMATH**
If this be true, I'll make thee Governor.      _LOL !_

**BARABAS**
And if it be not true, then let me die.

**CALYMATH**
Thou'st doomed thyself, assault it presently.      95

                                       *Exeunt*

78   *poppy ... mandrake* sleep-inducing potions
79   *belike* probably
80   *how else* somehow
81   *rests* waits
84   *against* near
      *sluice* ed. (Q truce)
87   *common channels* public sewers
95   *doomed* sentenced
      *presently* at once

# [ACT V, SCENE ii]

*Alarms. Enter* TURKS, BARABAS, [*with*] GOVERNOR [FERNEZE]
*and* KNIGHTS *prisoners*

CALYMATH

    Now vail your pride you captive Christians,
    And kneel for mercy to your conquering foe:
    Now where's the hope you had of haughty Spain?
    Ferneze, speak, had it not been much better
    To keep thy promise than be thus surprised?         5

FERNEZE

    What should I say, we are captives and must yield.

CALYMATH

    Ay, villains, you must yield, and under Turkish yokes
    Shall groaning bear the burden of our ire;
    And Barabas, as erst we promised thee,
    For thy desert we make thee Governor;         10
    Use them at thy discretion.

BARABAS               Thanks, my lord.

FERNEZE

    Oh fatal day to fall into the hands
    Of such a traitor and unhallowed Jew!
    What greater misery could heaven inflict?

CALYMATH

    'Tis our command: and Barabas, we give         15
    To guard thy person, these our Janizaries:
    Entreat them well, as we have usèd thee.
    And now, brave Bashaws, come, we'll walk about
    The ruined town, and see the wrack we made:
    Farewell brave Jew, farewell great Barabas.        20

---

   1    *vail* abase (see II.ii.11)
   5    *To keep* ed. (Q To kept)
   8    *ire* rage
   9    *erst* formerly
  10    *thee Governor;* ed. (Q the Governor,)
  11    *them* the captives
  16    *Janizaries* Turkish infantry. On the dangers of relying upon Janizaries, see Machia-
             velli, *The Prince* XVIII.
  17    *Entreat* Treat
  19    *wrack* destruction

*Exeunt* [CALYMATH *and* BASHAWS]

BARABAS

May all good fortune follow Calymath.
And now, as entrance to our safety,
To prison with the Governor and these
Captains, his consorts and confederates.

FERNEZE

Oh villain, heaven will be revenged on thee.                    25

*Exeunt* [TURKS *with* FERNEZE *and* KNIGHTS]

BARABAS

Away, no more, let him not trouble me.
Thus hast thou gotten, by thy policy,
No simple place, no small authority,
I now am Governor of Malta; true,
But Malta hates me, and in hating me                            30
My life's in danger, and what boots it thee
Poor Barabas, to be the Governor,
Whenas thy life shall be at their command?
No, Barabas, this must be looked into;
And since by wrong thou got'st authority,                       35
Maintain it bravely by firm policy,
At least unprofitably lose it not:
For he that liveth in authority,
And neither gets him friends, nor fills his bags,
Lives like the ass that Aesop speaketh of,                      40
That labours with a load of bread and wine,
And leaves it off to snap on thistle tops:
But Barabas will be more circumspect.
Begin betimes, Occasion's bald behind,

22    *entrance to our safety* first step in our security
31    *boots* avails
33    *Whenas* seeing that
      *at their command* subject to their disposition
34    *looked into* considered carefully
39    *bags* purse
40–2  The fable may not be from Aesop, but the proverbial point is clear enough: the
      donkey does not profit from his labours but eats common thistles (compare *Julius
      Caesar* IV.i.21–8).
44    *betimes* quickly
      *Occasion's bald behind* As traditionally depicted, Occasion or Opportunity is a figure
      who must be grabbed by her long forelock before she passes because the rest of her
      head is bald.

Slip not thine opportunity, for fear too late                    45
Thou seek'st for much, but canst not compass it.
Within here.

      *Enter* GOVERNOR [FERNEZE] *with a* GUARD

FERNEZE
  My lord?
BARABAS
  Ay, 'lord', thus slaves will learn.
  Now Governor stand by there – wait within –                    50

                               [*Exit* GUARD]

  This is the reason that I sent for thee;
  Thou seest thy life, and Malta's happiness,
  Are at my arbitrament; and Barabas
  At his discretion may dispose of both:
  Now tell me, Governor, and plainly too,                        55
  What think'st thou shall become of it and thee?
FERNEZE
  This; Barabas, since things are in thy power,
  I see no reason but of Malta's wrack,
  Nor hope of thee but extreme cruelty,
  Nor fear I death, nor will I flatter thee.                     60
BARABAS
  Governor, good words, be not so furious;
  'Tis not thy life which can avail me aught,
  Yet you do live, and live for me you shall:
  And as for Malta's ruin, think you not
  'Twere slender policy for Barabas                               65
  To dispossess himself of such a place?
  For sith, as once you said, within this isle

45   *Slip not* Do not let slip away
46   *compass* achieve       *it.* ed. (Q it)
47   *Within here* a summons
50   *there – wait within –* ed. (Q there, wait within,). Barabas appears to want Ferneze to
      stay and the guard to depart.
53   *arbitrament* disposal
58   *no reason but of* no alternative but
61   *good words* i.e. do not speak so fiercely
62   *avail me aught* do me any good
63   *Yet* still
      *for me* i.e. as far as I am concerned
65   *slender* slightly grounded, ill-considered
67   *sith* since

In Malta here, that I have got my goods,
And in this city still have had success,
And now at length am grown your Governor,                    70
Yourselves shall see it shall not be forgot:
For as a friend not known, but in distress,
I'll rear up Malta now remediless.

FERNEZE

Will Barabas recover Malta's loss?
Will Barabas be good to Christians?                          75

BARABAS

What wilt thou give me, Governor, to procure
A dissolution of the slavish bands
Wherein the Turk hath yoked your land and you?
What will you give me if I render you
The life of Calymath, surprise his men,                      80
And in an out-house of the city shut
His soldiers, till I have consumed 'em all with fire?
What will you give him that procureth this?

FERNEZE

Do but bring this to pass which thou pretendest,
Deal truly with us as thou intimatest,                       85
And I will send amongst the citizens
And by my letters privately procure
Great sums of money for thy recompense:
Nay more, do this, and live thou Governor still.

BARABAS

Nay, do thou this, Ferneze, and be free;                     90
Governor, I enlarge thee, live with me,
Go walk about the city, see thy friends:
Tush, send not letters to 'em, go thyself,
And let me see what money thou canst make;
Here is my hand that I'll set Malta free:                    95
And thus we cast it: to a solemn feast
I will invite young Selim-Calymath,

69    *still* continually
72    *as a friend not known, but in distress* as a friend who is unrecognized until the
      moment of need
79    *render* grant
81    *out-house* outlying building
84    *pretendest* put forward for consideration
91    *enlarge* free
96    *cast* plot

Where be thou present only to perform
One stratagem that I'll impart to thee,
Wherein no danger shall betide thy life,          100
And I will warrant Malta free for ever.

FERNEZE

Here is my hand, believe me, Barabas,
I will be there, and do as thou desirest;
When is the time?

BARABAS               Governor, presently.
For Calymath, when he hath viewed the town,      105
Will take his leave and sail toward Ottoman.

FERNEZE

Then will I, Barabas, about this coin,
And bring it with me to thee in the evening.

BARABAS

Do so, but fail not; now farewell Ferneze:

                    [*Exit* FERNEZE]

And thus far roundly goes the business:      110
Thus loving neither, will I live with both,
Making a profit of my policy;
And he from whom my most advantage comes,
Shall be my friend.
This is the life we Jews are used to lead;      115
And reason too, for Christians do the like:
Well, now about effecting this device:
First to surprise great Selim's soldiers,
And then to make provision for the feast,
That at one instant all things may be done,      120
My policy detests prevention:
To what event my secret purpose drives,
I know; and they shall witness with their lives.      *Exit*

---

100    *betide* happen to
101    *warrant* promise
106    *toward Ottoman.* ed. (Q toward, Ottoman,) i.e. Turkey
107    *about this coin* go about getting this money
110    *roundly* fairly, successfully
115    *used to* accustomed to
116    *And reason too* And with good reason
121    *prevention* being forestalled
122–3   The phrasing recalls that of Hieronimo's antagonist, Lorenzo, in *The Spanish Tragedy*
       III.iv.82–8.

# [ACT V, SCENE iii]

*Enter* CALYMATH, BASHAWS

CALYMATH

Thus have we viewed the city, seen the sack,
And caused the ruins to be new repaired,
Which with our bombards' shot and basilisks',
We rent in sunder at our entry:
And now I see the situation,                                         5
And how secure this conquered island stands
Environed with the Mediterranean Sea,
Strong countermured with other petty isles;
And toward Calabria backed by Sicily,
Two lofty turrets that command the town.                            10
When Syracusian Dionysius reigned;
I wonder how it could be conquered thus?

*Enter a* MESSENGER

MESSENGER

From Barabas, Malta's Governor, I bring
A message unto mighty Calymath;
Hearing his sovereign was bound for sea,                            15
To sail to Turkey, to great Ottoman,

---

1    *sack* plundering
3    *bombards* cannons of an early type, throwing large shot or stone
     *basilisks'* ed. (Q Basiliske) brass cannon
4–12  The order here printed preserves that of Q; the lineation of this speech has been
     much debated, with some editors arguing line 10 is misplaced and belongs between
     lines 4 and 5, with a substitution of 'where' for 'when' in line 11.
8    *countermured* ed. (Q contermin'd) defended
9    *toward Calabria backed by Sicily* in the direction of Calabria (in Italy) defended by
     Sicily
10   *lofty turrets* perhaps the forts of Saint Angelo and Saint Elmo
11   *Syracusian Dionysius* probably Dionysius I (c. 430–367 B.C.), tyrant of Syracuse and
     aggressive military leader; from Plato to the end of the sixteenth century, a figure
     standing for oppressive tyranny
11–12  'When' Dionysius reigned, Calymath reasons, the military-political advantages of
     imperial tyranny would have compounded Malta's natural impregnability, so could
     it really have been conquered this easily? The question mark may indicate a tone
     mixing wonder with something like a rhetorical question.
16   *great Ottoman* the sultan of Turkey

He humbly would entreat your majesty
To come and see his homely citadel,
And banquet with him ere thou leav'st the isle.

CALYMATH

To banquet with him in his citadel;                                        20
I fear me, messenger, to feast my train
Within a town of war so lately pillaged,
Will be too costly and too troublesome:
Yet would I gladly visit Barabas.
For well has Barabas deserved of us.                                       25

MESSENGER

Selim, for that, thus saith the Governor,
That he hath in store a pearl so big,
So precious, and withal so orient,
As be it valued but indifferently,
The price thereof will serve to entertain                                  30
Selim and all his soldiers for a month;
Therefore he humbly would entreat your highness
Not to depart till he has feasted you.

CALYMATH

I cannot feast my men in Malta walls,
Except he place his tables in the streets.                                  35

MESSENGER

Know, Selim, that there is a monastery
Which standeth as an out-house to the town;
There will he banquet them, but thee at home,
With all thy Bashaws and brave followers.

CALYMATH

Well, tell the Governor we grant his suit,                                 40
We'll in this summer evening feast with him.

---

18   *homely* simple, plain
20   *citadel*; ed. (Q Citadell,)
21   *train* retinue
22   *of* by
     *lately* recently
26   *for that* concerning that objection
27   *in store* in reserve
28   *withal* in addition
     *so orient* so lustrous
35   *Except* Unless

MESSENGER

    I shall, my lord.               *Exit*

CALYMATH

    And now bold Bashaws, let us to our tents,

    And meditate how we may grace us best

    To solemnize our Governor's great feast.       45

                        *Exeunt*

44   *meditate how we may grace* consider how we may equip

# [ACT V, SCENE iv]

*Enter* GOVERNOR [FERNEZE], KNIGHTS, [MARTIN] DEL BOSCO

FERNEZE
    In this, my countrymen, be ruled by me,
    Have special care that no man sally forth
    Till you shall hear a culverin discharged
    By him that bears the linstock, kindled thus;
    Then issue out and come to rescue me,          5
    For happily I shall be in distress,
    Or you releasèd of this servitude.

1 KNIGHT
    Rather than thus to live as Turkish thralls,
    What will we not adventure?

FERNEZE
    On then, begone.

KNIGHTS           Farewell grave Governor.          10

                                [*Exeunt*]

2   *sally forth* venture out
3   *culverin* an elongated cannon
4   *linstock* a staff holding the flame for igniting the charge
6   *happily* perchance
8   *thralls* slaves
9   *adventure* risk
10  KNIGHTS ed. (Q *Kni:*)
     *grave* respected

*tragic flaw - pride/greed*

# [ACT V, SCENE v]

*Enter [BARABAS] with a hammer above, very busy;*
*[and CARPENTERS]*

BARABAS
How stand the cords? How hang these hinges, fast?
Are all the cranes and pulleys sure?
CARPENTER                                          All fast.
BARABAS
Leave nothing loose, all levelled to my mind.
Why now I see that you have art indeed.
There, carpenters, divide that gold amongst you:          5
Go swill in bowls of sack and muscadine:
Down to the cellar, taste of all my wines. *poisoned*
CARPENTERS
We shall, my lord, and thank you.          *NOT PAY IN THE BILL!*

*Exeunt [CARPENTERS]*

BARABAS
And if you like them, drink your fill and die:
For so I live, perish may all the world.          10
Now Selim-Calymath return me word
That thou wilt come, and I am satisfied.

*Enter MESSENGER*

Now sirrah, what, will he come?
MESSENGER
He will; and has commanded all his men
To come ashore, and march through Malta streets,          15
That thou mayst feast them in thy citadel.

  1   *How stand* i.e. in what condition are
       *fast* secure
  2   CARPENTER ed. (Q *Serv.*)
  3   *levelled to my mind* in keeping with my plan
  6   *swill* drink (as an animal) greedily
       *bowls* drinking vessels
       *sack and muscadine* wines (Spanish and muscatel)
  9   *And if* If
       *die* Barabas has poisoned the wine.
  10  *so* provided that
  12  s.d. located after line 13 in Q

**BARABAS**

Then now are all things as my wish would have 'em,
There wanteth nothing but the Governor's pelf,

*Enter* GOVERNOR [FERNEZE]

And·see he brings it: now, Governor, the sum.

**FERNEZE**

With free consent a hundred thousand pounds.                    20

**BARABAS**

Pounds say'st thou, Governor? Well since it is no more
I'll satisfy myself with that; nay, keep it still,
For if I keep not promise, trust not me.
And Governor, now partake my policy:
First for his army they are sent before,                         25
Entered the monastery, and underneath
In several places are field-pieces pitched,
Bombards, whole barrels full of gunpowder,
That on the sudden shall dissever it,
And batter all the stones about their ears,                      30
Whence none can possibly escape alive:
Now as for Calymath and his consorts,
Here have I made a dainty gallery,
The floor whereof, this cable being cut,             plot/plan
Doth fall asunder; so that it doth sink                          35
Into a deep pit past recovery.
Here, hold that knife, and when thou seest he comes,
And with his Bashaws shall be blithely set,
A warning-piece shall be shot off from the tower,
To give thee knowledge when to cut the cord,                    40

TRUSTS
SOMEONE
   ELSE!
NO BUENO!!

---

18    *pelf* money, with possible depreciatory sense
18    s.d. located after line 19 in Q
21    *Governor? Well* ed. (Q Gouernor, well)
24    *partake* be acquainted with
27    *field-pieces pitched* light cannon readied
28    *Bombards* large cannon
29    *dissever it* blow up the monastery
32    *consorts* associates
33    *dainty* delightful
36    *past recovery* without escape
37    Barabas gives (throws?) the knife to Ferneze.
38    *blithely set* merrily seated at table
39    *warning-piece* signal gun

And fire the house; say, will not this be brave?

FERNEZE

Oh excellent! Here, hold thee, Barabas,
I trust thy word, take what I promised thee.

BARABAS

No, Governor, I'll satisfy thee first,
Thou shalt not live in doubt of any thing.                          45
Stand close, for here they come:

[FERNEZE *retires*]
                        why, is not this
A kingly kind of trade to purchase towns
By treachery, and sell 'em by deceit?
Now tell me, worldlings, underneath the sun,
If greater falsehood ever has been done.                           50

*Enter* CALYMATH *and* BASHAWS

CALYMATH

Come, my companion Bashaws, see I pray
How busy Barabas is there above
To entertain us in his gallery;
Let us salute him. Save thee, Barabas.

BARABAS

Welcome great Calymath.                                             55

FERNEZE

(How the slave jeers at him?)

BARABAS

Will't please thee, mighty Selim-Calymath,
To ascend our homely stairs?

CALYMATH

Ay, Barabas, come Bashaws, attend.

FERNEZE [*Coming forward*]           Stay, Calymath;
For I will show thee greater courtesy                               60
Than Barabas would have afforded thee.

---

41    *the house* the monastery
42    *hold thee* Ferneze offers Barabas money
46    *Stand close* Step aside into concealment
49–50    This boasting address to the audience under the name of 'worldlings' is strongly
          reminiscent of medieval drama.
49    *worldlings* those devoted to worldly pleasures or pursuits
       *sun* ed. (Q summe)
54    *salute him. Save* ed. (Q salute him, Saue)
       *Save thee* God save thee
58    *homely* simple, rude

KNIGHT
[*Within*] Sound a charge there.

*A charge [sounded], the cable cut, a cauldron*
*discovered [into which* BARABAS *falls]*

[*Enter* MARTIN DEL BOSCO *and* KNIGHTS]

CALYMATH
How now, what means this?

BARABAS
Help, help me, Christians, help.

FERNEZE
See Calymath, this was devised for thee.                    65

CALYMATH
Treason, treason Bashaws, fly.

FERNEZE
No, Selim, do not fly;
See his end first, and fly then if thou canst.

BARABAS
Oh help me, Selim, help me Christians.
Governor, why stand you all so pitiless?                    70

GOVERNOR
Should I in pity of thy plaints or thee,
Accursèd Barabas, base Jew, relent?
No, thus I'll see thy treachery repaid,
But wish thou hadst behaved thee otherwise.

BARABAS
You will not help me then?

FERNEZE                          No, villain, no.         75

BARABAS
And villains, know you cannot help me now.
Then Barabas breathe forth thy latest fate,
And in the fury of thy torments, strive

---

62   *charge* trumpet signal for attack
     s.d. *discovered* revealed. Ferneze cuts the rope, opening the trapdoor which Barabas
     has constructed over the cauldron. As Hunter has suggested, the fall into the cauld-
     ron strongly recalls representations of sinners' punishment in hell. It is appropriate
     that Barabas suffer the punishment for avarice.
63   *this?* ed. (Q this)
71   *plaints* expressions of sorrow and injury
72   *Accursèd Barabas, base Jew, relent?* ed. (Q Accursed *Barabas;* base Jew relent:)
77   *latest* last

129

To end thy life with resolution:
Know, Governor, 'twas I that slew thy son; 80
I framed the challenge that did make them meet:
Know, Calymath, I aimed thy overthrow,
And had I but escaped this stratagem,
I would have brought confusion on you all,
Damned Christians, dogs, and Turkish infidels; 85
But now begins the extremity of heat
To pinch me with intolerable pangs:
Die life, fly soul, tongue curse thy fill and die! [Dies]

CALYMATH
Tell me, you Christians, what doth this portend?

GOVERNOR
This train he laid to have entrapped thy life; 90
Now Selim note the unhallowed deeds of Jews:
Thus he determined to have handled thee,
But I have rather chose to save thy life.

CALYMATH
Was this the banquet he prepared for us?
Let's hence, lest further mischief be pretended. 95

FERNEZE
Nay, Selim, stay, for since we have thee here,
We will not let thee part so suddenly:
Besides, if we should let thee go, all's one,
For with thy galleys could'st thou not get hence,
Without fresh men to rig and furnish them. 100

CALYMATH
Tush, Governor, take thou no care for that,
My men are all aboard,
And do attend my coming there by this.

FERNEZE
Why heard'st thou not the trumpet sound a charge?

79   *resolution* fortitude
82   *aimed* intended
84   *confusion* destruction
87   *pinch* torment, torture
89   *portend* mean
90   *train* plot
92   *determined* planned
95   *pretended* intended
98   *all's one* it would not make any difference
103  *attend . . . this* anticipate my return at this time

CALYMATH

  Yes, what of that?

FERNEZE               Why then the house was fired,      105

  Blown up and all thy soldiers massacred.

CALYMATH

  Oh monstrous treason!

FERNEZE               A Jew's courtesy:

  For he that did by treason work our fall,

  By treason hath delivered thee to us:

  Know therefore, till thy father hath made good      110

  The ruins done to Malta and to us,

  Thou canst not part: for Malta shall be freed,

  Or Selim ne'er return to Ottoman.

CALYMATH

  Nay rather, Christians, let me go to Turkey,

  In person there to meditate your peace;      115

  To keep me here will nought advantage you.

FERNEZE

  Content thee, Calymath, here thou must stay,

  And live in Malta prisoner; for come call the world

  To rescue thee, so will we guard us now,

  As sooner shall they drink the ocean dry,      120

  Than conquer Malta, or endanger us.

  So march away, and let due praise be given

  Neither to fate nor fortune, but to heaven.

                           [*Exeunt*]

*FINIS*

108   *work our fall* achieve our downfall
109   *treason* treachery
115   *meditate* plan
116   *nought advantage* do you no good
118   *come call the world* were all the world to come
123   *fate ... fortune ... heaven* Ferneze rejects alternative causalities in favour of Christian Providence. Whatever other ironies this may carry in the context of the play, it is potentially significant that he rejects the notion of fortune's sway, since Machiavelli's emphasis on fortune is such a focus in anti-Machiavellian polemic.

# APPENDIX
## 'THE DUTCH CHURCH LIBEL'

Concern about widespread hostility to the 'stranger' community (which numbered about 5,000, or about 4 to 5% of the London populace in the late sixteenth century) and its threat to the peace appears in documentary evidence drawn from every level of Elizabethan government – alder-manic reports, Recorder Fleetwood's investigations, the Lord Mayor's warnings, records of the Privy Council, Parliamentary proceedings – and the evidence spans the period of composition and production of Marlowe's play.[1] A recently discovered document, which may itself have contributed to the legal difficulties of both Kyd and Marlowe in May 1593, may compactly illustrate the salient terms of popular resentment in the late 1580s and early 1590s.

In May of 1593, the anonymous 'Dutch Church Libel' was appended to one of the foreign Protestant churches in London, warning 'Ye strangers yt doe inhabite in this lande' to 'expect . . . such a fatall day' as that which had disastrously befallen the Huguenot community at the hands of Catholic forces in the 'Paris massacre' of 1572. The charges of this document suggest the atmosphere in which *The Jew of Malta* was written and produced, and they also lend remarkable contemporary implication to Marlowe's play and especially to its representation of Barabas. The abuses attributed to the foreigners by the libel are numerous, but particularly interesting in relation to the play are the following associations: with merchant practices that are called Machiavellian ('Your Machiavellian Marchant spoyles the state') and involve international marketing, decep-tive retailing, employing an uprooted underclass as agents and substit-uting showy 'gawds' for intrinsically valuable 'goods'; with usury ('Your vsery doth leave vs all for deade') and with pursuing more than a single means of livelihood ('every merchant hath three trades at least'); with greedy depredation that is likened to the ritual Jewish cannibalism of anti-Semitic lore ('like the Jewes, you eate vs vp as bread') in taking wealth from the impoverished English ('with our store continually you feast'); with religious hypocrisy ('in counterfeitinge religion') and with an insu-lar Jewish zealotry ('in your temples praying'); with displacing the native poor to a mercenary military service on their behalf ('our pore soules, are cleane thrust out of dore / And to the warres are sent abroade . . . / as

---

1 See Archer, *Pursuit of Stability*, pp. 4–5, 132; Pettegree, *Foreign Protestant Communities*, pp. 219f.

A Libell fixt vpon the French Church Wall, in London. Anno. 1593.

Ye strangers yt doe inhabite in this lande
Note this same writing doe it vnderstand
Conceit it well for safegard of your lyves
your goods, your children, & your dearest wives
Your Machiavellian Marchant spoyles the state,
your Vsery doth leave vs all for deade
your Artifex, & craftesman works our fate,
And like the Jewes, you eate vs vp as bread
The Marchant doth ingrosse all kinde of wares
Forestall's the markets, wheresoere he goes
Sends forth his wares, by pedlers to the faiers,
Retayl's at home, & with his horrible showes:       Conto's th thousandes
In Baskets your wares trott vp & downe
Carried the streets by the country nation
you are intelligencers to the state & crowne
And in your harts doe wish an alteration,
you transport goods, & bring vs gawds good store
Our Leade, our Vittaile, our Ordenance & what nott
That Egipts plagues, vext not the Egyptians more
Then you doe vs; then death shall be your lotte
Noe prize comes in but you make claime therto
And every merchant hath three trades at least
And Cutthrote like in selling you vndoe
vs all, & with our store continually you feast:  We cannot suffer long.
Our poore artificers doe starve & dye
For yt they cannot growe be sett on worke
And for your worke more curious to the eye
In Chambers, twenty in one house will lurke,
Raysing of rents, was never knowne before
Liuing farre better then at native home
And our poore soules, are cleane thrust out of dores
And to the warres are sent abroade to rome,
To fight it out for Fraunce & Belgia,
And dy like dogges as sacrifice for you
Expect you therefore such a fatall day
Shortly on you, & yours for to ensewe: as never was seene.
Since words nor threats nor any other thinge
canne make you to avoyd this certaine ill
Weele cutt your throtes, in your temples praying
Not paris massacre so much blood did spill
As we will doe iust vengeance on you all
In counterfeiting religion for your flight
When t'is well knowne, you are loth, for to be thrall

The Bodleian Library, Oxford, MS Don. d., 152, fol. 4

134

sacrifice for you'); with both spying for the government ('You are intelligencers to the state & crown') and with desires for social 'alteracion', or,
alternatively, with representing a financial internationalism that threatens
'our gracious Queene' by corrupting the English nobility ('With Spanish
gold, you all are infected / And with yt gould our Nobles wink').

The text which follows is that transcribed by Arthur Freeman from
Bodleian Ms. Don. d. 152, and it is reprinted from his 'Marlowe, Kyd, and
the Dutch Church Libel' (*ELR* 3 (1973), 44–51) by permission of the
editors. Freeman provides an account of the Libel (the names 'French'
and 'Dutch' for the two churches were often confused) and its relation to
anti-stranger violence as well as to the legal difficulties of Marlowe and
Thomas Kyd in 1593.

A Libell, fixte vpon the French Church Wall, in London. Anno 1593.

Ye strangers yt doe inhabite in this lande
Note this same writing doe it vnderstand
Conceit it well for savegard of your lyves
Your goods, your children, & your dearest wives
Your Machiavellian Marchant spoyles the state,
Your vsery doth leave vs all for deade
Your Artifex, & craftesman works our fate,
And like the Jewes, you eate us vp as bread
The Marchant doth ingross all kinde of wares
Forestall's the markets, whereso 'ere he goe's
Sends forth his wares, by Pedlers to the faires,
Retayle's at home, & with his horrible showes:      Vndoeth thowsands
In Baskets your wares trott up & downe
Carried the streets by the country nation,
You are intelligencers to the state & crowne
And in your hartes doe wish an alteracion,
You transport goods, & bring vs gawds good store
Our Leade, our Vittaile, our Ordenance & what nott
That Egipts plagues, vext not the Egyptians more
Then you doe vs; then death shall be your lotte
Noe prize comes in but you make claime therto
And every merchant hath three trades at least,
And Cutthroate like in selling you vndoe
vs all, & with our store continually you feast:      We cannot suffer long.
Our pore artificers doe starve & dye
For yt they cannot now be sett on worke

And for your worke more curious to the ey[.]
In Chambers, twenty in one house will lurke,
Raysing of rents, was never knowne before
Living farre better then at native home
And our poore soules, are cleane thrust out of dore
And to the warres are sent abroade to rome,
To fight it out for Fraunce & Belgia,
And dy like dogges as sacrifice for you
Expect you therefore such a fatall day
Shortly on you, & yours for to ensewe:          as never was seene.
Since words nor threates not any other thinge
canne make you to avoyd this certaine ill
Weele cutt your throtes, in your temples praying
Not paris massacre so much blood did spill
As we will doe iust vengeance on you all
In counterfeitinge religion for your flight
When 't'is well knowne, you are loth, for to be thrall
your coyne, & you as countryes cause to flight
With Spanish gold, you all are infected
And with yt gould our Nobles wink at feats
Nobles said I? nay men to be reiected,
Upstarts yt enioy the noblest seates
That wound their Countries brest, for lucres sake
And wrong our gracious Queene & Subiects good
By letting strangers make our harts to ake
For which our swords are whet, to shedd their blood
And for a truth let it be vnderstood/        Fly, Flye, & never returne.
per. Tamberlaine

# NOTES